The Most Precious Message:

THE INFINITE GIFT OF CALVARY

The Most Precious Message:

THE INFINITE GIFT OF CALVARY

Martin Klein

ISBN: 978-0-9975897-4-0 (paperback)

Religion: Christian Life: Inspirational

Back cover references:

[1] E. G. White, *Manuscript 77-1899*.23

[2] E. G. White, *The Ellen G. White 1888 Materials* (1987), p. 1452.1, 1452.3.

[3] E. G. White, *Heavenly Places* (1967), p. 42.5.

[4] E. G. White, *Testimonies for the Church* (1889), Vol. 5, 346.1.

[5] E. G. White, *Daughters of God* (1998), p. 221.3.

The author assumes full responsibility for the accuracy and interpretation of the E. G. White quotations cited in this book.

www.savannahpictures.com

Dedicated to those sin-sick souls who long for truth but have yet to experience that peace and healing to be found nowhere else than in Jesus Christ; to whom the Great Physician gives the invitation: "Come unto me all ye that labor and are heavy laden and I will give you rest."

Table of Contents

Introduction

"The thought that the righteousness of Christ is imputed to us, not because of any merit on our part, but as a free gift from God, is a precious thought. The enemy of God and man is not willing that this truth should be clearly presented; for he knows that if the people receive it fully, his power will be broken."[1]

"We need also much more knowledge; we need to be enlightened in regard to the plan of salvation. There is not one in one hundred who understands for himself the Bible truth on this subject that is so necessary to our present and eternal welfare. When light begins to shine forth to make clear the plan of redemption to the people, the enemy works with all diligence that the light may be shut away from the hearts of men. If we come to the Word of God with a teachable, humble spirit, the rubbish of error will be swept away, and gems of truth, long hidden from our eyes, will be discovered."[2]

"The Lord in His great mercy sent a most precious message to His people.... This message was to bring more prominently before the world [1]**the uplifted Saviour**, the [2]**sacrifice for the sins of the whole world**. It presented [3]**justification through faith in the Surety**; it [4]**invited** the people to receive the [5]**righteousness** of Christ, **which is made manifest in obedience** to all the commandments of God.
"[6]**Many had lost sight of Jesus**. They needed to have their eyes directed to [7]**His divine person**, [8]**His merits**, and [9]**His changeless love** for the human family. [10]**All power is given into His hands**, that He may dispense rich gifts unto men, imparting the [11]**priceless gift of His own righteousness** to [12]**the helpless human agent**. This is the message that God commanded to be given to the world. It is [13]**the third angel's message**, which is to be **proclaimed with a loud voice**, and attended with [14]**the outpouring of His Spirit** in a large measure."[3]

---

[1] E. G. White, *The Faith I Live By* (Washington D.C.: Review and Herald Publishing Association, 1958), p. 111.6

[2] E. G. White, *Selected Messages* (Washington D.C.: Review and Herald Publishing Association, 1958), Vol. 1, p. 359.2.

[3] E. G. White, *Last Day Events* (Boise, ID: Pacific Press Publishing Association, 1992) p. 200.1-2.

"'God so loved the world, that he gave his only begotten Son, that whosoever believeth in him should not perish, but have everlasting life.' Calvary is the estimate that heaven has placed upon the human soul. God gave Jesus, the richest gift of heaven, to pay the ransom price for the human family."[4]

"To the death of Christ we owe even this earthly life. The bread we eat is the purchase of His broken body. The water we drink is bought by His spilled blood. Never one, saint or sinner, eats his daily food, but he is nourished by the body and the blood of Christ. The cross of Calvary is stamped on every loaf. It is reflected in every water spring."[5]

"If you give yourself to him, and accept him as your Saviour, then, sinful as your life may have been, for his sake you are accounted righteous. Christ's character stands in place of your character, and you are accepted before God just as if you had not sinned."[6]

---

[4] E. G. White, *The Review and Herald*, May 22, 1894, par. 1

[5] E. G. White, *The Desire of Ages* (Nampa, ID: Pacific Press Publishing Co., 1898), p. 660.3.

[6] E. G. White, *The Review & Herald,* November 11, 1915 par. 2.

1. The Uplifted Saviour

"In the year that king Uzziah died" the prophet Isaiah "saw also the Lord sitting upon a throne, high and lifted up, and his train filled the temple. Above it stood the seraphims: each one had six wings; with twain [two] he covered his face, and with twain he covered his feet, and with twain he did fly. And one cried unto another, and said, Holy, holy, holy, is the LORD of hosts: the whole earth is full of his glory. And the posts of the door moved at the voice of him that cried, and the house was filled with smoke. Then said I, Woe is me! for I am undone; because I am a man of unclean lips, and I dwell in the midst of a people of unclean lips: for mine eyes have seen the King, the LORD of hosts."[1]

Isaiah was given a glimpse of the exalted position of Christ the king, the Lord of hosts.[2] He saw Christ on a throne, in the temple of heaven, high and lifted up. The angels surrounding him proclaim his holiness. When the prophet Isaiah saw the exaltation of Christ he said, "Woe is me! for I am undone."

"This was a revelation of the glory of Christ's divinity. Note the humility of the seraphim before him. With their wings they veiled their faces and their feet. They were in the presence of Jesus. They saw the glory of God,—the King in his beauty,—and they covered themselves...."[3]

The majesty of Jesus Christ is inexpressible in human language. So very dim is our conception of the brightness and glory of the Son of God. It is when the Saviour is uplifted before the world that sinners will be drawn to his beauty. The power of the Protestant Reformation was in the uplifted Saviour. In exalted language, the famed Erasmus, the first to print the Bible in the original tongue, correcting the errors of the Latin Vulgate,[4] lifts up Jesus: "Who in all history, is like to Jesus, ineffably, inconceivably God of God, born before all times,

---

[1] Isaiah 6:1-5

[2] See chapter seven: *His Divinity*.

[3] E. G. White, *The Review and Herald,* February 18, 1896 par. 2.

[4] E. G. White, *The Great Controversy* (Nampa, ID: Pacific Press Publishing Co., 1911), p. 245.1.

eternal and fully equal to his eternal and loftiest parent? Does not his human birth easily overshadow that of all kings? By the will of the Father and the breath of the Spirit he was born of a Virgin, a man in time and still God, unsullied by our corruption. Who is richer than he who gives all things and is not diminished? Who more illustrious as the splendor of the glory of the Father, enlightening every man that comes into the world? Who more powerful than he to whom the Father has given power in heaven and on earth? Who more mighty by whose nod the universe was established? at whose nod the sea is calm... diseases flee, armed men fall on their faces, devils are expelled, rocks rent, the dead raised, sinners repent, and all things are made new? Who is more august whom angels adore and before whom devils tremble? Who more invincible than he who has conquered death and cast down Satan from heaven? Who more triumphant than he who has harrowed hell and brought souls to heaven where he sits at the right hand of God the Father? Who is more wise than he who founded and governs the universe in harmony? Whose authority is greater than his of whom the Father said, 'This is my beloved Son. Hear ye him?' Who is more to be feared than he who can cast body and soul into hell? Who more fair than he whom to behold is perfect joy? Who is more ancient than he who has no beginning and will have no end? But perhaps [we] may better think of him as a boy, lying in swaddling clothes in a manger, while angels sang, shepherds adored, the animals knew him, the star stood over where he lay, Herod trembled, Simeon embraced, Hanna prophesied. O humble simplicity! O sublime humility! How can thoughts conceive or words suffice to express his greatness? Better to adore than to seek to explain. What then shall we do, if John the Baptist said he was unworthy to unloose the latchet of his shoes? Strive... to sit at the feet of Jesus the teacher."[5]

None in all the universe is more exalted than Jesus: "Wherefore God also hath highly exalted him, and given him a name which is above every name: That at the name of Jesus every knee should bow, of things in heaven, and things in earth, and things under the earth; And that every tongue should confess that Jesus Christ is Lord, to the glory of God the Father."[6]

---

[5] Roland Bainton, *Erasmus of Christendom* (New York: Charles Scribner's Sons, 1969), p. 102.

[6] Philippians 2:9-11

Christ is exalted above all others and yet the Bible records simply: "Who, being in the form of God, thought it not robbery to be equal with God: But made himself of no reputation, and took upon him the form of a servant, and was made in the likeness of men: And being found in fashion as a man, he humbled himself, and became obedient unto death, even the death of the cross."[7] Though he was the majesty of heaven he was willing to condescend to this dark world in the form of a man. In a rude building that stabled the cattle, the Redeemer of the world, the King of glory, was born.

"The story of Bethlehem is an exhaustless theme. In it is hidden 'the depth of the riches both of the wisdom and knowledge of God.' Romans 11:33. We marvel at the Saviour's sacrifice in exchanging the throne of heaven for the manger, and the companionship of adoring angels for the beasts of the stall. Human pride and self-sufficiency stand rebuked in His presence. Yet this was but the beginning of His wonderful condescension. It would have been an almost infinite humiliation for the Son of God to take man's nature, even when Adam stood in his innocence in Eden. But Jesus accepted humanity when the race had been weakened by four thousand years of sin. Like every child of Adam He accepted the results of the working of the great law of heredity. What these results were is shown in the history of His earthly ancestors. He came with such a heredity to share our sorrows and temptations, and to give us the example of a sinless life."[8]

Jesus left the courts of glory and joined the human race that he might save you. "I present before you the life of self-denial, humility, and sacrifice of our divine Lord. The Majesty of heaven, the King of glory, left His riches, His splendor, His honor and glory, and, in order to save sinful man, condescended to a life of humility, poverty, and shame; 'who for the joy that was set before Him endured the cross, despising the shame.'"[9]

"Who can comprehend the love here displayed! The angelic host beheld with wonder and with grief Him who had been the Majesty of heaven, and who had worn the crown of glory, now wearing the

---

[7] Philippians 2:6-8

[8] E. G. White, *The Desire of Ages* (1898), p. 48.5.

[9] E. G. White, *Testimonies for the Church* (Mountain View, CA: Pacific Press Publishing Association, 1871), Vol. 2, p. 490.2.

crown of thorns, a bleeding victim to the rage of an infuriated mob, fired to insane madness by the wrath of Satan. Behold the patient Sufferer! Upon His head is the thorny crown. His lifeblood flows from every lacerated vein. All this in consequence of sin! Nothing could have induced Christ to leave His honor and majesty in heaven, and come to a sinful world, to be neglected, despised, and rejected by those He came to save, and finally to suffer upon the cross, but eternal, redeeming love, which will ever remain a mystery. "Wonder, O heavens, and be astonished, O earth! Behold the oppressor and the oppressed! A vast multitude enclose the Saviour of the world. Mockings and jeerings are mingled with the coarse oaths of blasphemy. His lowly birth and humble life are commented upon by unfeeling wretches. His claim to be the Son of God is ridiculed by the chief priests and elders, and vulgar jests and insulting derision are passed from lip to lip.... Christ, the precious Son of God, was led forth, and the cross was laid upon His shoulders. At every step was left blood which flowed from His wounds. Thronged by an immense crowd of bitter enemies and unfeeling spectators, He is led away to the crucifixion. 'He was oppressed, and He was afflicted, yet He opened not His mouth: He is brought as a lamb to the slaughter, and as a sheep before her shearers is dumb, so He openeth not His mouth.'"[10]

Jesus said "And I, if I be lifted up from the earth, will draw all men unto me. This he said, signifying what death he should die."[11] In another place he says, "When ye have lifted up the Son of man, then shall ye know that I am he ..."[12]

But, "with many the story of the condescension, humiliation, and sacrifice of our divine Lord awakens no deeper interest, and stirs the soul and affects the life no more, than does the history of the death of the martyrs of Jesus. Many have suffered death by slow tortures; others have suffered death by crucifixion. In what does the death of God's dear Son differ from these? It is true He died upon the cross a most cruel death; yet others, for His dear sake, have suffered equally, so far as bodily torture is concerned. Why, then, was the suffering of Christ more dreadful than that of other persons who have

[10] E. G. White, *Testimonies for the Church* (1871), Vol. 2, p. 207.1-2.

[11] John 12:32-33

[12] John 8:28

yielded their lives for His sake? If the sufferings of Christ consisted in physical pain alone, then His death was no more painful than that of some of the martyrs."[13] "The sufferings of martyrs can bear no comparison with the sufferings of Christ. The divine presence was with them, in their physical sufferings. There was the hiding of the Father's face from his dear Son."[14] "Bodily pain was but a small part of the agony of God's dear Son. The sins of the world were upon Him, also the sense of His Father's wrath as He suffered the penalty of the law transgressed. It was these that crushed His divine soul. It was the hiding of His Father's face—a sense that His own dear Father had forsaken Him—which brought despair. The separation that sin makes between God and man was fully realized and keenly felt by the innocent, suffering Man of Calvary. He was oppressed by the powers of darkness. He had not one ray of light to brighten the future. And He was struggling with the power of Satan, who was declaring that he had Christ in his power, that he was superior in strength to the Son of God, that the Father had disowned His Son, and that He was no longer in the favor of God any more than himself. If He was indeed still in favor with God, why need He die? God could save Him from death."[15] "Oh, was there ever suffering and sorrow like that endured by the dying Saviour! It was the sense of His Father's displeasure which made His cup so bitter. It was not bodily suffering which so quickly ended the life of Christ upon the cross. It was the crushing weight of the sins of the world, and a sense of His Father's wrath. The Father's glory and sustaining presence had left Him, and despair pressed its crushing weight of darkness upon Him and forced from His pale and quivering lips the anguished cry: 'My God, My God, why hast Thou forsaken Me?'"[16]

In his interview with Nicodemus, Jesus made the connection between the serpent on the pole in the wilderness and his death, when he said, "And as Moses lifted up the serpent in the wilderness, even so must the Son of man be lifted up: That whosoever believeth in him should not perish, but have eternal life. For God so loved the

---

[13] E. G. White, *Testimonies for the Church* (1871), Vol. 2, p. 214.1.

[14] E. G. White, *The Signs of the Times*, August 14, 1879, par. 12.

[15] E. G. White, *Testimonies for the Church* (1871), Vol. 2, p. 214.2.

[16] *Ibid.*, p. 209.1.

world, that he gave his only begotten Son, that whosoever believeth in him should not perish, but have everlasting life."[17]

As the children of Israel journeyed on toward Canaan they became discouraged with the way and began to complain to God that there was no bread or water and that they were tired of the manna that God had mercifully provided for them. Because of their unbelief and murmuring, God's protection was removed which allowed deadly reptiles to infest the camp resulting in the death of many. When the people cried unto Moses confessing that they had sinned against the Lord, "the LORD said unto Moses, Make thee a fiery serpent, and set it upon a pole: and it shall come to pass, that every one that is bitten, when he looketh upon it, shall live. And Moses made a serpent of brass, and put it upon a pole, and it came to pass, that if a serpent had bitten any man, when he beheld the serpent of brass, he lived."[18] "Look unto me, and be ye saved, all the ends of the earth: for I am God, and there is none else. "[19]

"Moses was bidden to lift the brazen serpent on the pole, and make the proclamation that whosoever should look upon it should live. And all who looked, did live. They recovered health at once... What a strange symbol of Christ was that likeness of the serpents which stung them."[20]

Why was Christ symbolized by a serpent—normally the representation of Satan and sin? Scripture says,"For he hath made him to be sin for us, who knew no sin; that we might be made the righteousness of God in him."[21] "Who his own self bare our sins in his own body on the tree, that we, being dead to sins, should live unto righteousness."[22] On the cross of Calvary Christ hung as the sin-bearer and became sin for us. Thus he is represented as a

---

[17] John 3:14-16

[18] Numbers 21:8-9

[19] Isaiah 45:22

[20] E. G. White, *Sons and Daughters of God* (Washington, D.C.: Review and Herald Publishing Association, 1955), p. 222.2.

[21] 2 Corinthians 5:21

[22] 1 Peter 2:24

serpent. As Moses lifted up the serpent in the wilderness, in the same manner the Son of man was lifted up on the cross, becoming sin that we might become the righteousness of God in him.

"His love for the fallen race, His desire to save them, was so great that He took upon Himself the wrath of His Father, and consented to suffer the penalty of that transgression which plunged guilty man in degradation. He bore the sins of man in His own body. 'He hath made Him to be sin for us, who knew no sin; that we might be made the righteousness of God in Him.'"[23]

"As Moses lifted up the serpent in the wilderness, so has the Son of man been lifted up, that whosoever looks unto him in faith, may not perish, but have everlasting life. Look to Jesus, uplifted on the cross. When the serpent was lifted upon the pole in the camp of Israel, the proclamation went forth that all who were bitten by the fiery serpents were to look to that brazen symbol; and whoever looked was immediately healed. The people were not to reason how this was possible, not to question wherein was the virtue to make them whole. They were to do exactly as they were bidden. Those who stopped to reason, died. Just so we are to look to Jesus; sinful, erring, weak, unworthy, we are to take the word of God, the invitation of Christ: 'Come unto me, all ye that labor and are heavy laden, and I will give you rest. Take my yoke upon you, and learn of me; for I am meek and lowly in heart; and ye shall find rest unto your souls. For my yoke is easy, and my burden is light.'"[24]

John the Baptist, on the banks of the Jordan, when he saw Jesus cried, "Behold the Lamb of God, which taketh away the sin of the world."[25] Behold the Lamb of God! Behold the uplifted Savior dying for your sins. "His visage was so marred more than any man, and his form more than the sons of men...

"Who hath believed our report? and to whom is the arm of the LORD revealed?... He is despised and rejected of men; a man of sorrows, and acquainted with grief: and we hid as it were our faces from him; he was despised, and we esteemed him not. Surely he hath borne our griefs, and carried our sorrows: yet we did esteem him stricken,

---

[23] E. G. White, *Testimonies for the Church* (1868), Vol. 1, p. 482.2.

[24] E. G. White, *The Signs of the Times*, August 1, 1895, par. 16.

[25] John 1:29

smitten of God, and afflicted. But he was wounded for our transgressions, he was bruised for our iniquities: the chastisement of our peace was upon him; and with his stripes we are healed."[26]

"The world's Redeemer was treated as we deserve to be treated, in order that we might be treated as he deserved to be treated. He came to our world and took our sins upon his own divine soul, that we might receive his imputed righteousness. He was condemned for our sins, in which he had no share, that we might be justified by his righteousness, in which we had no share. The world's Redeemer gave himself for us. Who was he?—The Majesty of heaven, pouring out his blood upon the altar of justice for the sins of guilty man."[27]
Jesus Christ, the Majesty of heaven, the King of the universe—loves you so much that he was willing to come and be lifted up on a tree; to gather all your sin upon his own divine soul; to become sin for you; to receive the wrath of God against sin; to suffer the penalty for your transgression, so that you might become the righteousness of God in him. God proposes to treat you as the King of the universe deserved to be treated.[28] "Oh, what love, what matchless love! Christ, the Son of God, dying for guilty man!"[29]

"The same healing, life-giving message is now sounding. It points to the uplifted Saviour upon the shameful tree. Those who have been bitten by that old serpent, the devil, are bidden to look and live... Look alone to Jesus as your righteousness and your sacrifice. As you are justified by faith, the deadly sting of the serpent will be healed."[30]

"Jesus cares for each one as though there were not another individual on the face of the earth.... The Majesty of heaven held not Himself aloof from degraded, sinful humanity. We have not a high priest who is so high, so lifted up, that He cannot notice us or

---

[26] Isaiah 52:14-53:5

[27] E. G. White, *The Review and Herald*, March 21, 1893, par. 6.

[28] Revelation 3:21

[29] E. G. White, *Selected Messages* (1980), Vol. 3, p. 193.4.

[30] E. G. White, *The Ellen G. White 1888 Materials* (Washington, D.C.: Ellen G. White Estate, 1987), p. 1452.1, 1452.3.

The Uplifted Saviour

sympathize with us, but one who was in all points tempted like as we are, yet without sin."[31]

"Let us remember that our great High Priest is pleading before the mercy seat in behalf of his ransomed people. He ever liveth to make intercession for us. If any man sin, we have an advocate with the Father, Jesus Christ the righteous. The blood of Jesus is pleading with power and efficacy for those who are backslidden, for those who are rebellious, for those who sin against great light and love. Satan stands at our right hand to accuse us, and our advocate stands at God's right hand to plead for us. He has never lost a case that has been committed to him."[32]

"Wherefore he is able also to save them to the uttermost that come unto God by him, seeing he ever liveth to make intercession for them. For such an high priest became us, who is holy, harmless, undefiled, separate from sinners, and made higher than the heavens."[33] "Seeing then that we have a great high priest, that is passed into the heavens, Jesus the Son of God, let us hold fast our profession. For we have not an high priest which cannot be touched with the feeling of our infirmities; but was in all points tempted like as we are, yet without sin. Let us therefore come boldly unto the throne of grace, that we may obtain mercy, and find grace to help in time of need."[34]

"Without the cross, man could have no union with the Father. On it depends our every hope. From it shines the light of the Saviour's love; and when at the foot of the cross the sinner looks up to the One who died to save him, he may rejoice with fulness of joy; for his sins are pardoned. Kneeling in faith at the cross, he has reached the highest place to which man can attain."[35]

---

[31] E. G. White, *Testimonies for the Church* (1889), Vol. 5, 346.1.

[32] E. G. White, *The Review and Herald,* August 15, 1893, par. 7.

[33] Hebrews 7:25-26

[34] Hebrews 4:14-16

[35] E. G. White, *Sons and Daughters of God* (1955), p. 222.2-4.

2. His Sacrifice for the Sins of the Whole World

"The soul that sinneth, it shall die,"[1] "for the wages of sin is death."[2] None have escaped; none are exempt. "For all have sinned, and come short of the glory of God;"[3] "there is none righteous, no, not one:...They are all gone out of the way, they are together become unprofitable; there is none that doeth good, no, not one."[4] "We are all as an unclean thing, and all our righteousnesses are as filthy rags; and we all do fade as a leaf; and our iniquities, like the wind, have taken us away."[5] Of ourselves our condition is hopeless; all seems lost. "This was the position of the human race after man divorced himself from God by transgression. Then he was no longer entitled to a breath of air, a ray of sunshine, or a particle of food. And the reason why man was not annihilated was because God so loved him that He made the gift of His dear Son that He should suffer the penalty of his transgression."[6]

"The broken law of God demanded the life of the sinner. In all the universe there was but one who could, in behalf of man, satisfy its claims. Since the divine law is as sacred as God Himself, only one equal with God could make atonement for its transgression. None but Christ could redeem fallen man from the curse of the law and bring him again into harmony with Heaven."[7]

"Therefore as by the offence of one judgment came upon all men to condemnation; even so by the righteousness of one"—the infinite virtue of Jesus Christ—"the free gift came upon all men unto justification of life."[8] Just as the sin of Adam brought judgment upon

---

[1] Ezekiel 18:20

[2] Romans 6:23

[3] Romans 3:23

[4] Romans 3:10-12

[5] Isaiah 64:6

[6] E. G. White, *Faith and Works* (Nashville, TN: Southern Publishing Association, 1979), p. 21.1-2.

[7] E. G. White, *Patriarchs and Prophets* (Washington, D.C.: Review and Herald Publishing Association, 1890), p. 63.2.

[8] Romans 5:18

all men, "even so," or in the same way, the righteousness of Jesus made provision for the salvation of the race through justification of life. According to Scripture there is an aspect of justification that the sacrifice of Christ accomplished for all men, whether they know it, like it, believe it, accept it, or not. It is called justification of life.

Since the wages of sin is death, when Adam sinned, justice demanded that he be taken out behind the tree of life and shot. Each one of us, the very first time we sin, should be executed. How is it that we are still alive? Scripture calls Jesus "the Lamb slain from the foundation of the world."[9] The promise of Christ's sacrifice on our behalf was great enough to stay the execution of the sentence of justice, "who hath saved us, and called us with an holy calling, not according to our works, but according to his own purpose and grace, which was given us in Christ Jesus before the world began."[10] We deserve nothing but death; anything more that we possess, is because of the mercy and grace of the sacrifice of Jesus. "When we were sinners against God, and there was no hope for us, Christ consented to take our transgression on His soul. There was no virtue, no righteousness in us, that God should accept our efforts to keep the law. The provision was made before the foundation of the world that if transgression should enter, Christ would become our Substitute and Surety. The moment man fell in consequence of sin, that moment Christ was willing to take its consequences upon His soul. From that moment the sin of the world was laid upon Him. When God gave His Son he gave all heaven, that Satan could not say He could have done more than He had done for the human race."[11]

"To the death of Christ we owe even this earthly life. The bread we eat is the purchase of His broken body. The water we drink is bought by His spilled blood. Never one, saint or sinner, eats his daily food, but he is nourished by the body and the blood of Christ. The cross of Calvary is stamped on every loaf. It is reflected in every water spring."[12]

---

[9] Revelation 13:8

[10] 2 Timothy 1:9. See also 1 Peter 1:18-20; Ephesians 1:4.

[11] E. G. White, *Experiences in Australia* (Silver Spring, MD: Ellen G. White Estate, 2015), p. 158.4.

[12] E. G. White, *The Desire of Ages* (1898), p. 660.3.

Every breath of air inhaled by the most heaven-daring, blasphemous sinner comes from the sacrifice of God. Every nourishment the infidel consumes is paid for by the blood of Jesus. All the energy and materials needed for the atheist to war against God is provided by the blood of his Creator.

"Hating sin with a perfect hatred, he yet gathered to his soul the sins of the whole world, as he trod the path to Calvary, suffering the penalty of the transgressor. Guiltless, he bore the punishment of the guilty; innocent, yet offering himself to bear the penalty of the transgression of the law of God. The punishment of the sins of every soul was borne by the Son of the infinite God. The guilt of every sin pressed its weight upon the divine soul of the world's Redeemer. He who knew no sin became sin for us, that we might be made the righteousness of God in him. In assuming the nature of man, he placed himself where he was wounded for our transgressions, bruised for our iniquities, that by his stripes we might be healed."[13]

"To wit, that God was in Christ, reconciling the world unto himself, not imputing their trespasses unto them; and hath committed unto us the word of reconciliation."[14] "Reconciliation means that every barrier between the soul and God is removed, and that the sinner realizes what the pardoning love of God means. By reason of the sacrifice made by Christ for fallen men, God can justly pardon the transgressor who accepts the merits of Christ. Christ was the channel through which the mercy, love, and righteousness might flow from the heart of God to the heart of the sinner. 'He is faithful and just to forgive us our sins, and to cleanse us from all unrighteousness.' (1 John 1:9)."[15] Impute means to assign. God the Father, therefore, has restored all mankind to friendly relations with himself by the death of Jesus, and has not assigned our sins to us, because the punishment for every sin ever committed, or ever to be committed, was borne by the infinite sacrifice of the Son of God. God has committed to Christians "the ministry of reconciliation"—the duty of telling sinners that the free gift of God has come upon them, that they have been restored to right relations with God by the sacrifice of Jesus, therefore he is not imputing their trespasses to them.

---

[13] E. G. White, *The Review and Herald,* December 20, 1892 par 6.

[14] 2 Corinthians 5:19

[15] E. G. White, *Selected Messages* (1958), Vol. 1, p. 395.2.

"But God commendeth his love toward us, in that, while we were yet sinners, Christ died for us. Much more then, being now justified by his blood, we shall be saved from wrath through him. For if, when we were enemies, we were reconciled to God by the death of his Son, much more, being reconciled, we shall be saved by his life."[16] According to Scripture, Christ reconciled the entire world to himself, while we were yet his enemies. Therefore, God has already reconciled, by his death, those that are still his enemies.

"We have an advocate with the Father, Jesus Christ the righteous: And he is the propitiation for our sins: and not for ours only, but also for the sins of the whole world."[17] "In this was manifested the love of God toward us, because that God sent his only begotten Son into the world, that we might live through him. Herein is love, not that we loved God, but that he loved us, and sent his Son to be the propitiation for our sins."[18] According to Scripture, the death of Christ was not only the payment for the sins of the believer, but also for the sins of the entire planet. "We see Jesus, who was made a little lower than the angels for the suffering of death, crowned with glory and honour; that he by the grace of God should taste death for every man."[19]

Many a sinner, bowed down with the weight of their guilt, wonders if their confession was good enough; if they had enough faith for God to forgive; if they made themselves miserable for long enough to prove to God that they were sorry. It is impossible to know something that is not a fact—something that is not true. In order for something to be known it must already be true. We could never know with certainty that our debt of sin is paid unless it is already a fact. This is why the fact of salvation was made known to Adam and Eve as soon as they sinned: "And I will put enmity between thee and the woman, and between thy seed and her seed; it shall bruise thy head, and thou shalt bruise his heel."[20] The promise of a saviour, to be born a descendant of the woman, who would crush the head of the serpent,

[16] Romans 5:8-10

[17] 1 John 2:1-2

[18] 1 John 4:9-10

[19] Hebrews 2:9

[20] Genesis 3:15

but who would receive a deadly bite in the process gave the guilty pair a glimmer of hope through the tears of remorse and dull ache of the knowledge of their death sentence. "But of the tree of the knowledge of good and evil, thou shalt not eat of it: for in the day that thou eatest thereof thou shalt surely die."[21] As Adam's unwilling hands slit the throat of the first sacrificial victim, his Creator clothed the now naked couple with a white garment of lamb's skin, replacing the inadequate fig leaf garment of self justification.[22] In the death of that first bleeding lamb Adam glimpsed the promise of an innocent substitute that would die in his place, "the Lamb slain from the foundation of the world."[23] Isaiah gave the same prophetic message, that the LORD would be revealed through the coming Messiah who would be "despised and rejected of men; a man of sorrows, and acquainted with grief: and we hid as it were our faces from him; he was despised, and we esteemed him not. Surely he hath borne our griefs, and carried our sorrows: yet we did esteem him stricken, smitten of God, and afflicted. But he was wounded for our transgressions, he was bruised for our iniquities: the chastisement of our peace was upon him; and with his stripes we are healed. All we like sheep have gone astray; we have turned every one to his own way; and the LORD hath laid on him the iniquity of us all. He was oppressed, and he was afflicted, yet he opened not his mouth: he is brought as a lamb to the slaughter, and as a sheep before her shearers is dumb, so he openeth not his mouth."[24] Upon this sacrificial victim the LORD would lay "the iniquity of us all."

This does not mean that every sinner will be saved. Though the guilt and punishment of every person's sin was borne by the sacrifice of Christ, and he is therefore no longer imputing their sins unto them; the sinner must believe that the payment is sufficient to pay his debt. There are two aspects to justification: justification of life and justification by faith. The whole world has been given justification of life whether they know it, like it, believe it, accept it, or not, but only those who accept what his death already accomplished for them, and take his life in place of their own, are justified by faith.

---

[21] Genesis 2:17

[22] Genesis 3:9-21

[23] Revelation 13:8

[24] Isaiah 53:3-7

To illustrate this: My wife and I had a neighbor who lost their dog one night. To make a long story short, the next morning I went searching for and found the dog. They were so happy and thankful to us for finding the dog that they gave us a check for $400 dollars. My wife felt bad for taking $400 dollars from them since after all we were happy to help and would have done it for nothing. She said, "Let's just not cash it," and was about to shred it. But I said, "Wait! Don't shred it! It's not a check; it's a money order!" The difference between a check and a money order is that a check is only a promise of money—it could be invalid—but a money order is as good as cash. If you do not cash a check the person is never out the money. But if you do not cash a money order, the bank is probably happy, but the person that gave you the money order has already paid for that money order. God wrote a money order with his own blood to pay your debt. If you do not believe the value of the money order, it can never be applied to your debt. Why not trust him and cash it? You can shred it, but he still spent it.

Jesus Christ "loved us, and washed us from our sins in his own blood."[25] "Who will have all men to be saved, and to come unto the knowledge of the truth. For there is one God, and one mediator between God and men, the man Christ Jesus; Who gave himself a ransom for all, to be testified in due time."[26]

He has paid the penalty for your sins already—all of them! His sacrifice was for the sins of the whole world. That means he paid even for Hitler's sins. Christ died for the sins of the whole world, but not in a generic sense; in dying for the whole world he died for every individual. He died for you—whoever you are, whatever you have done.

"In His promises and warnings, Jesus means me. God so loved the world, that He gave His only-begotten Son, that I by believing in Him, might not perish, but have everlasting life. The experiences related in God's word are to be my experiences. Prayer and promise, precept and warning, are mine. 'I am crucified with Christ: nevertheless I live; yet not I, but Christ liveth in me: and the life which I now live in the

---

[25] Revelation 1:5

[26] 1 Timothy 2:4-6

flesh I live by the faith of the Son of God, who loved me, and gave Himself for me.'"[27]

"By pledging His own life Christ has made Himself responsible for every man and woman on the earth. He stands in the presence of God, saying, 'Father, I take upon Myself the guilt of that soul. It means death to him if he is left to bear it. If he repents he shall be forgiven. My blood shall cleanse him from all sin. I gave My life for the sins of the world.'"[28]

"Oh, was there ever suffering and sorrow like that endured by the dying Saviour! It was the sense of His Father's displeasure which made His cup so bitter. It was not bodily suffering which so quickly ended the life of Christ upon the cross. It was the crushing weight of the sins of the world, and a sense of His Father's wrath. The Father's glory and sustaining presence had left Him, and despair pressed its crushing weight of darkness upon Him and forced from His pale and quivering lips the anguished cry: 'My God, My God, why hast Thou forsaken Me?'"[29]

The majesty of the universe became one with the human family, calling us brethren, and walking the path of this vale of woe for us, feeling every grief we have ever borne. "As our substitute and surety, he felt every pang of anguish that we can ever feel. He himself suffered, being tempted."[30] "In all their affliction he was afflicted, and the angel of his presence saved them: in his love and in his pity he redeemed them; and he bare them, and carried them all the days of old."[31]

"The Elder Brother of our race is by the eternal throne. He looks upon every soul who is turning his face toward Him as the Saviour. He knows by experience what are the weaknesses of humanity, what

---

[27] E. G. White, *The Desire of Ages* (1898), p. 390.5.

[28] E. G. White, *In Heavenly Places* (Washington D.C.: Review and Herald Publishing Association, 1967), p. 42.5.

[29] E. G. White, *Testimonies for the Church* (1871), Vol. 2, p. 209.1

[30] E. G. White, *The Review and Herald,* October 2, 1900 par 11.

[31] Isaiah 63:9

are our wants, and where lies the strength of our temptations; for He was in all points tempted like as we are, yet without sin."[32]

"Jesus was sinless and had no dread of the consequences of sin. With this exception His condition was as yours. You have not a difficulty that did not press with equal weight upon Him, not a sorrow that His heart has not experienced. His feelings could be hurt with neglect, with indifference of professed friends, as easily as yours. Is your path thorny? Christ's was so in a tenfold sense. Are you distressed? So was He. How well fitted was Christ to be an example!"[33] "Jesus once stood in age just where you now stand. Your circumstances, your cogitations at this period of your life, Jesus has had. He cannot overlook you at this critical period. He sees your dangers. He is acquainted with your temptations. He invites you to follow His example."[34]

God shows us a glorious mystery: Christ became one with the human race, yet as its divine head he became the infinite representative of the race. "For such an high priest became us, who is holy, harmless, undefiled, separate from sinners, and made higher than the heavens."[35] Thus he carried every pain, every sin, every injustice—felt every sorrow, and suffered every abuse. "If one died for all, then were all dead."[36] Christ died an infinite death that was the punishment of all of us, offering every descendent of Adam the option of eternal life. "They shall call his name Emmanuel, which being interpreted is, God with us.[37]

"Herein is the mystery of redemption, that the innocent, pure, and holy Son of the infinite God was permitted to bear the punishment of a thankless race of rebels against the divine government; that through the manifestation of His matchless love, these rebels might

---

[32] E. G. White, *The Desire of Ages* (1898), p. 329.1.

[33] Hebrews 7:26

[34] E. G. White, *Manuscript Releases* (Silver Spring, MD: Ellen G. White Estate, 1990), Vol. 4, p. 235.2.

[35] Hebrews 7:26

[36] 2 Corinthians 5:14

[37] Matthew 1:21-23

be inspired with faith in, and love for God, and might stand before Him repentant, forgiven, guiltless, as if they had never sinned. Angels in heaven marveled that the wrath of God should be laid on His well-beloved Son; that a life of infinite value in the heavenly courts should be given for the worthless life of a race degraded by sin."[38]

"It was Satan's purpose to bring about an eternal separation between God and man; but in Christ we become more closely united to God than if we had never fallen. In taking our nature, the Saviour has bound Himself to humanity by a tie that is never to be broken. Through the eternal ages He is linked with us. 'God so loved the world, that He gave His only-begotten Son.' John 3:16. He gave Him not only to bear our sins, and to die as our sacrifice; He gave Him to the fallen race. To assure us of His immutable counsel of peace, God gave His only-begotten Son to become one of the human family, forever to retain His human nature. This is the pledge that God will fulfill His word. 'Unto us a child is born, unto us a son is given: and the government shall be upon His shoulder.' God has adopted human nature in the person of His Son, and has carried the same into the highest heaven. It is the 'Son of man' who shares the throne of the universe. It is the 'Son of man' whose name shall be called, 'Wonderful, Counselor, The mighty God, The everlasting Father, The Prince of Peace.' Isaiah 9:6. The I AM is the Daysman between God and humanity, laying His hand upon both. He who is 'holy, harmless, undefiled, separate from sinners,' is not ashamed to call us brethren. Hebrews 7:26; 2:11. In Christ the family of earth and the family of heaven are bound together. Christ glorified is our brother. Heaven is enshrined in humanity, and humanity is enfolded in the bosom of Infinite Love."[39]

"The Sinless One has taken our place. 'The Lord hath laid on Him the iniquity of us all.' Isaiah 53:6. He has borne the burden of our guilt. He will take the load from our weary shoulders. He will give us rest..."[40]

---

[38] E. G. White, *The Bible Echo*, November 25, 1895 par. 5.

[39] E. G. White, *The Desire of Ages* (1898), p. 25.3.

[40] E. G. White, *The Desire of Ages* (1898), p. 328.5. See also *The Review and Herald*, July 19, 1892 par. 1; April 17, 1894 par. 7; May 18, 1897 par. 4-5.

"Man has not been made a sin-bearer, and he will never know the horror of the curse of sin which the Saviour bore. No sorrow can bear any comparison with the sorrow of Him upon whom the wrath of God fell with overwhelming force."[41]

"'He was wounded for our transgressions, he was bruised for our iniquities: the chastisement of our peace was upon him; and with his stripes we are healed.' This penalty Christ bore for the sins of the transgressor; He has borne the punishment for every man and for this reason He can ransom every soul, however fallen his condition, if he will accept the law of God as his standard of righteousness."[42]

"It is your privilege to believe that Christ has borne your sins; for God hath laid on Him the iniquity of us all. You are under the shelter of the sure refuge, under the cover of the atoning blood of the acceptable sacrifice.
"All legalism, all the sorrow and woe by which you may encompass yourself, will not give you one moment of relief. You cannot rightly estimate sin. You must accept God's estimate, and it is heavy indeed. If you bore the guilt of your sin, it would crush you; but the sinless One has taken your place, and though undeserving, He has borne your guilt. By accepting the provision God has made, you may stand free before Him in the merit and virtue of your Substitute."[43]
Christ bore your sins—your personal sins. "His own self bare our sins in his own body on the tree,"[44] "being made a curse for us."[45] "Christ took upon Himself the condemnation of sin. He opened His bosom to the woes of man... As man's substitute and surety, the iniquity of men was laid upon Christ; He was counted a transgressor that He might redeem them from the curse of the law.... He, the Sin-Bearer, endures judicial punishment for iniquity and becomes sin itself for man."[46]

---

[41] E. G. White, *That I May Know Him*, p. 64.2-4.

[42] E. G. White, *S.D.A Bible Commentary* (Washington, D.C.: Review and Herald Publishing Association, 1955) Vol. 4, p. 1147.5.

[43] E. G. White, The *Bible Echo*, July 2, 1894 par. 2-3. *See also* Signs of the Times, February 27, 1893 par. 4.

[44] 1 Peter 2:24

[45] Galatians 3:13

[46] E. G. White, *The Faith I Live By* (1958), p. 104.4-5.

"Justice demands that sin be not merely pardoned, but the death penalty must be executed. God, in the gift of His only-begotten Son, met both these requirements. By dying in man's stead, Christ exhausted the penalty and provided a pardon."[47] "Here is where thousands fail; they do not believe that Jesus pardons them personally, individually. They do not take God at His word. It is the privilege of all who comply with the conditions to know for themselves that pardon is freely extended for every sin. Put away the suspicion that God's promises are not meant for you. They are for every repentant transgressor. Strength and grace have been provided through Christ to be brought by ministering angels to every believing soul. None are so sinful that they cannot find strength, purity, and righteousness in Jesus, who died for them. He is waiting to strip them of their garments stained and polluted with sin, and to put upon them the white robes of righteousness; He bids them live and not die."[48]

God came as a man and poured out his soul unto death; he spilled his blood to pay that money order; he risked the entire universe to save you. There is no higher price that could be paid to purchase your salvation. In his death he exhausted the penalty and provided a pardon. There is nothing more for you to pay. "Christ drank the bitter draught to the very dregs. He was not spared one pang of anguish."[49] You do not have to humiliate or cause yourself pain to lessen your guilt. There is nothing you can do to gain his forgiveness, but to accept it.

God reconciled the world unto himself and therefore does not impute your sins to you. Your sins are already paid for. God now pleads with you to accept the money order. He says, Wait! Don't shred it! It is of infinite value! I poured out my life blood for your salvation! All of heaven has been paid for your sins! You may "have redemption through his blood, even the forgiveness of sins."[50]

---

[47] E. G. White, *S.D.A. Bible Commentary* (1956), Vol. 6, p. 1099.2.

[48] E. G. White, *Steps to Christ* (Mountain View, CA: Pacific Press Publishing Association, 1892), p. 52.3.

[49] E. G. White, *The Signs of the Times*, August 9, 1905 par. 5.

[50] Colossians 1:14

"If we confess our sins, he is faithful and just to forgive us our sins, and to cleanse us from all unrighteousness."[51] All we must do is confess that we have a debt that needs to be paid. When we confess we no longer have to wonder, did I make a good enough confession?; was I sorry enough?; did I afflict myself enough so that God will know that I'm really sorry and forgive me? Pop psychology claims you just need to forgive yourself. This is a blasphemous doctrine of devils, for "Who can forgive sins, but God alone?"[52] We do not have to try to forgive ourselves; we cannot forgive ourselves! The death of Christ has paid the price for your forgiveness. God has provided pardon for you. Will you not accept it? Will you not cash his money order?

The sacrifice has already been made, which means that our confession of our sins is simply an acknowledgment that we have a debt. Faith is "the evidence of things not seen"[53]—not the things themselves. We do not make something true by having enough faith; faith simply believes facts—it responds to what God has already done or promised. When we confess that we have sinned and are in need of forgiveness; in need of the money order, Jesus says to us, "be of good cheer; thy sins be forgiven thee."[54] "The grace of Christ is freely to justify the sinner without merit or claim on his part. Justification is a full, complete pardon of sin. The moment a sinner accepts Christ by faith, that moment he is pardoned. The righteousness of Christ is imputed to him, and he is no more to doubt God's forgiving grace."[55]

"The sin of the whole world was laid upon Jesus, and divinity gave its highest value to the suffering of humanity in Jesus, that the whole world might be pardoned through faith in the Substitute. The most guilty need have no fear that God will not pardon, for because of the

[51] 2 Corinthians 5:19-21

[52] Luke 5:21

[53] Hebrews 11:1

[54] Matthew 9:2

[55] E. G. White, The Signs of the Times, May 19, 1898, par. 11.

efficacy of the divine sacrifice the penalty of the law will be remitted. Through Christ the sinner may return to allegiance to God."[56]

The sins of whole world may be paid for; salvation for every soul purchased; yet not all will be saved. "For as by one man's disobedience many were made sinners, so by the obedience of one shall many be made righteous."[57] Not all are made righteous. Not all will take his life. Not all will cash the money order. Not all believe that it has value. What happens if you reject the money order—the infinite price paid for your forgiveness? "Blessed are they whose iniquities are forgiven, and whose sins are covered. Blessed is the man to whom the Lord will not impute sin."[58] Since there is a man who is blessed because the Lord does not impute sin to him, that means by definition that there must be a man who is not blessed (cursed) because the Lord does impute sin unto him. Jesus describes this by parable in Matthew 18: "Therefore is the kingdom of heaven likened unto a certain king, which would take account of his servants. And when he had begun to reckon, one was brought unto him, which owed him ten thousand talents. But forasmuch as he had not to pay, his lord commanded him to be sold, and his wife, and children, and all that he had, and payment to be made. The servant therefore fell down, and worshipped him, saying, Lord, have patience with me, and I will pay thee all. Then the lord of that servant was moved with compassion, and loosed him, and forgave him the debt. But the same servant went out, and found one of his fellowservants, which owed him an hundred pence:[59] and he laid hands on him, and took him by the throat, saying, Pay me that thou owest. And his fellowservant fell down at his feet, and besought him, saying, Have patience with me, and I will pay thee all. And he would not: but went and cast him into prison, till he should pay the debt. So when his fellowservants saw what was done, they were very sorry, and came and told unto their lord all that was done. Then his lord, after that he had called him, said unto him, O thou wicked servant, I forgave thee all that debt, because thou desiredst me: Shouldest not thou also

---

[56] E. G. White, *The Faith I Live By* (1958), p. 104.9.

[57] Romans 5:8-10

[58] Romans 4:7-8

[59] One hundred pence was about 4.5 months of wages for a common worker. In today's economy this is perhaps about $7,000-$8,000. At this rate of payment per year it would take almost 60 years to pay off the debt of ten thousand talents, assuming no interest.

have had compassion on thy fellowservant, even as I had pity on thee? And his lord was wroth, and delivered him to the tormentors, till he should pay all that was due unto him. So likewise shall my heavenly Father do also unto you, if ye from your hearts forgive not every one his brother their trespasses."[60]

The king reconciles the accounts of his servants, and finds one who has a very large debt—so large that the servant cannot possibly pay it; at the very minimum $400 million.[61] To pay the debt, his life was to be required in servitude. However, when he pleads with the king, claiming he would repay all, his Lord simply forgave his entire debt. Apparently, he did not really believe that he was forgiven, for he immediately went and found someone who owed him and tried to collect money from that man—ostensibly to help pay back his own debt. When his lord heard, he commanded that he should be delivered to the tormentors, till he should pay all that was due. His debt was imputed back to him.

Therefore, in the judgement, every man is judged, condemned, and punished "according to his works."[62] Even though each sin of every individual was borne by the spotless Son of God, if the person fails to apply that provision to their debt, refusing to acknowledge its existence, the debt will remain. God has provided everything for our salvation, but if we reject all that he has done and hold onto our sins he cannot save us. He will not violate our freedom of choice. God values our freedom more than he values our salvation.

"For God sent not his Son into the world to condemn the world; but that the world through him might be saved. He that believeth on him is not condemned: but he that believeth not is condemned already, because he hath not believed in the name of the only begotten Son of God. And this is the condemnation, that light is come into the world, and men loved darkness rather than light, because their deeds were evil."[63]

---

[60] Matthew 18:23-35

[61] "Ten thousand talents... at the lowest computation, amounts to not less than fifteen million dollars." E. G. White, *Manuscript Releases* (1990), Vol. 15, p. 186.3.
Fifteen million dollars in 1888 would be approximately $400 million today.

[62] Proverbs 24:12; Matthew 16:27

[63] John 3:17-19

"Christ is able to save to the uttermost all who come to Him in faith. He will cleanse them from all defilement if they will let Him. But if they cling to their sins, they cannot possibly be saved; for Christ's righteousness covers no sin unrepented of. God has declared that those who receive Christ as their Redeemer, accepting Him as the One who takes away all sin, will receive pardon for their transgressions. These are the terms of our election. Man's salvation depends upon his receiving Christ by faith. Those who will not receive Him lose eternal life because they refused to avail themselves of the only means provided by the Father and the Son for the salvation of a perishing world."[64]

"Christ felt much as sinners will feel when the vials of God's wrath shall be poured out upon them. Black despair, like the pall of death, will gather about their guilty souls, and then they will realize to the fullest extent the sinfulness of sin. Salvation has been purchased for them by the suffering and death of the Son of God. It might be theirs, if they would accept of it willingly, gladly; but none are compelled to yield obedience to the law of God. If they refuse the heavenly benefit and choose the pleasures and deceitfulness of sin, they have their choice, and at the end receive their wages, which is the wrath of God and eternal death. They will be forever separated from the presence of Jesus, whose sacrifice they had despised. They will have lost a life of happiness and sacrificed eternal glory for the pleasures of sin for a season."[65]

Many today, hold in their hands an uncashed money order of infinite value which they are about to shred. Will you not accept the most precious gift ever given?

---

[64] E. G. White, *S.D.A Bible Commentary* (1957), Vol. 7, p. 931.1.

[65] E. G. White, *Testimonies for the Church* (1871), Vol. 2, p. 210.1.

The Most Precious Message

34

3. Justification Through Faith in the Surety

When a son walks into the car dealership to purchase his first car, his signature means very little to the car salesman. The signature of his father likely carries more weight. On the merit of the father's signature, the new car is purchased. The father becomes surety for the debt of his son. The father has guaranteed that the debt of his son will be paid. The father reasonably expects that the son will not proceed to abuse this surety and forge his father's signature to accrue more debt. The action of the father provides motivation for the conscientious son to treat the new car carefully. A valuable race horse could not co-sign the loan of the son's car, for it is not a human. The surety must be provided by a human with more authority and status than the son, and with more resources than the value of the debt.

"Man's substitute and surety must have man's nature, a connection with the human family whom He was to represent, and, as God's ambassador, He must partake of the divine nature, have a connection with the Infinite, in order to manifest God to the world, and be a mediator between God and man."[1]

"By so much was Jesus made a surety of a better testament."[2] "Be surety for thy servant for good: let not the proud oppress me. Mine eyes fail for thy salvation, and for the word of thy righteousness. Deal with thy servant according unto thy mercy, and teach me thy statutes."[3]

"[Christ] is our substitute and surety; He stands in the place of humanity, so that He Himself is affected as His weakest follower is affected. Such is the sympathy of Christ, which never allows Him to be an indifferent spectator of any suffering caused to His children. Not the slightest wound can be given by word, spirit, or action, that does not touch the heart of Him who gave His life for fallen humanity. Let us bear in mind that Christ is the great heart from which the lifeblood flows to every organ in the body. He is the head, from which

---

[1] E. G. White, *S.D.A. Bible Commentary* (1970), Vol. 7a, p. 488.4-5.

[2] Hebrews 7:22

[3] Psalms 119:122-124

extends every nerve to the minutest and remotest member of the body. When one member of that body with which Christ is so mysteriously connected, suffers, the throb of pain is felt by our Saviour."[4]

On the cross there was a battle fought that was the culmination of a life of victory. The battle raged for the gain or loss of the human race. "Forasmuch then as the children are partakers of flesh and blood, he also himself likewise took part of the same; that through death he might destroy him that had the power of death, that is, the devil; And deliver them who through fear of death were all their lifetime subject to bondage. For verily he took not on him the nature of angels; but he took on him the seed of Abraham. Wherefore in all things it behoved him to be made like unto his brethren, that he might be a merciful and faithful high priest in things pertaining to God, to make reconciliation for the sins of the people. For in that he himself hath suffered being tempted, he is able to succour them that are tempted."[5]

"Christ yielded not in the least degree to the torturing foe, even in His bitterest anguish. Legions of evil angels were all about the Son of God, yet the holy angels were bidden not to break their ranks and engage in conflict with the taunting, reviling foe. Heavenly angels were not permitted to minister unto the anguished spirit of the Son of God. It was in this terrible hour of darkness, the face of His Father hidden, legions of evil angels enshrouding Him, the sins of the world upon Him, that the words were wrenched from His lips: 'My God, My God, why hast Thou forsaken Me?'"[6]

"Nature sympathized with the suffering of its Author. The heaving earth, the rent rocks, proclaimed that it was the Son of God who died. There was a mighty earthquake. The veil of the temple was rent in twain. Terror seized the executioners and spectators as they beheld the sun veiled in darkness, and felt the earth shake beneath them, and saw and heard the rending of the rocks. The mocking and jeering of the chief priests and elders were hushed as Christ

---

[4] E. G. White, *Welfare Ministry* (Washington, D.C.: Review and Herald Publishing Association, 1952), p. 23.2.

[5] Hebrews 2:14-18

[6] E. G. White, *Testimonies for the Church* (1871), Vol. 2, p. 214.2-3.

commended His spirit into the hands of His Father. The astonished throng began to withdraw and grope their way in the darkness to the city. They smote upon their breasts as they went and in terror, speaking scarcely above a whisper, said among themselves: 'It is an innocent person that has been murdered. What if, indeed, He is, as He asserted, the Son of God?'

"Jesus did not yield up His life till He had accomplished the work which He came to do, and exclaimed with His departing breath: 'It is finished.' Satan was then defeated. He knew that his kingdom was lost. Angels rejoiced as the words were uttered: 'It is finished.' The great plan of redemption, which was dependent on the death of Christ, had been thus far carried out. And there was joy in heaven that the sons of Adam could, through a life of obedience, be finally exalted to the throne of God. Oh, what love! What amazing love! that brought the Son of God to earth to be made sin for us, that we might be reconciled to God, and elevated to a life with Him in His mansions in glory. Oh, what is man, that such a price should be paid for his redemption!"[7]

"Christ received His death wound, which was the trophy of His victory, and the victory of all who believe in Him. These wounds annihilated the power of Satan over every loyal, believing subject in Jesus Christ. By the suffering and death of Christ, human intelligences, fallen because of the sin of Adam, are through their acceptance of Christ and faith in Him, elevated to become heirs of immortality and an eternal weight of glory. The gates of the heavenly Paradise are thrown open to the inhabitants of this fallen world. Through faith in the righteousness of Christ, rebels against the law of God may lay hold upon the Infinite, and become partakers of everlasting life."[8]

"If you give yourself to him, and accept him as your Saviour, then, sinful as your life may have been, for his sake you are accounted righteous. Christ's character stands in place of your character, and you are accepted before God just as if you had not sinned."[9] Justification is more than simply a declaration made in heaven that you are righteous when you are not; it is not a legal matter that takes

---

[7] E. G. White, *Testimonies for the Church* (1871), Vol. 2, p. 211.1-2.

[8] E. G. White, *S.D.A. Bible Commentary* (1970), Vol. 7a, p. 466.5.

[9] E. G. White, *The Review & Herald*, November 11, 1915 par. 2.

place in heaven alone without a change taking place within you. When Christ declares that you are righteous in him, you are at that moment righteous in God's sight.

"The Holy Spirit ever abides with him who is seeking for perfection of Christian character. The Holy Spirit furnishes the pure motive, the living, active principle, that sustains striving, wrestling, believing souls in every emergency and under every temptation. The Holy Spirit sustains the believer amid the world's hatred, amid the unfriendliness of relatives, amid disappointment, amid the realization of imperfection, and amid the mistakes of life. Depending upon the matchless purity and perfection of Christ, the victory is sure to him who looks unto the Author and Finisher of our faith. We shall be more that conquerors through him who hath loved us, and given himself for us. He has borne our sins, in order that through him we might have moral excellence, and attain unto the perfection of Christian character. Our Righteousness is our substitute and surety."[10]

"And it came to pass on a certain day, as he was teaching, that there were Pharisees and doctors of the law sitting by, which were come out of every town of Galilee, and Judaea, and Jerusalem: and the power of the Lord was present to heal them. And, behold, men brought in a bed a man which was taken with a palsy: and they sought means to bring him in, and to lay him before him. And when they could not find by what way they might bring him in because of the multitude, they went upon the housetop, and let him down through the tiling with his couch into the midst before Jesus."[11]

"When Jesus saw their faith, he said unto the sick of the palsy, Son, thy sins be forgiven thee. But there were certain of the scribes sitting there, and reasoning in their hearts, Why doth this man thus speak blasphemies? who can forgive sins but God only? And immediately when Jesus perceived in his spirit that they so reasoned within themselves, he said unto them, Why reason ye these things in your hearts? Whether is it easier to say to the sick of the palsy, Thy sins be forgiven thee; or to say, Arise, and take up thy bed, and walk? But that ye may know that the Son of man hath power on earth to forgive

---

[10] E. G. White, *The Review & Herald*, November 30, 1897, par. 10.

[11] Luke 5:17-19

sins, (he saith to the sick of the palsy,) I say unto thee, Arise, and take up thy bed, and go thy way into thine house. And immediately he arose, took up the bed, and went forth before them all; insomuch that they were all amazed, and glorified God, saying, We never saw it on this fashion."[12]

Jesus said, "That ye may know that the Son of man has power to forgive sins," and said to the paralytic, "Arise, and take up thy bed, and go thy way into thine house." Jesus healed the paralytic that we might know that he has the power to forgive sins. The act of Jesus healing the paralytic was an illustration of how a man is forgiven and made right with God. "[I]t was not physical restoration he desired so much as relief from the burden of sin. If he could see Jesus, and receive the assurance of forgiveness and peace with Heaven, he would be content to live or die, according to God's will. The cry of the dying man was, Oh that I might come into His presence!"[13]

"The Saviour looked upon the mournful countenance, and saw the pleading eyes fixed upon Him. He understood the case; He had drawn to Himself that perplexed and doubting spirit. While the paralytic was yet at home, the Saviour had brought conviction to his conscience. When he repented of his sins, and believed in the power of Jesus to make him whole, the life-giving mercies of the Saviour had first blessed his longing heart. Jesus had watched the first glimmer of faith grow into a belief that He was the sinner's only helper, and had seen it grow stronger with every effort to come into His presence.
"Now, in words that fell like music on the sufferer's ear, the Saviour said, 'Son, be of good cheer; thy sins be forgiven thee.'
"The burden of despair rolls from the sick man's soul; the peace of forgiveness rests upon his spirit, and shines out upon his countenance. His physical pain is gone, and his whole being is transformed. The helpless paralytic is healed! the guilty sinner is pardoned!

---

[12] Mark 2:5-12

[13] E. G. White, *The Desire of Ages* (1898), p. 267.4.

"In simple faith he accepted the words of Jesus as the boon of new life. He urged no further request, but lay in blissful silence, too happy for words."[14]

The provision was already made for his healing when Jesus said to him, "arise and walk." But when Jesus told him to arise and walk he had to believe that he was healed, accept the word of Christ, act upon it, and rise in obedience to that command in order to experience the miracle of healing. If he had doubted whether it was possible; if he had said, I don't think Jesus can really heal me, therefore, I will not obey his command; if he had said, I can't get up because I deserve to be a paralytic since it was my sin that caused the disease, he could not experience the miracle of healing.

The death of Christ has paid the price for our sins. But when Jesus tells us the truth that our debt has been paid we must believe it is the case, accept the word of Christ, confess that we need his forgiveness, act upon his word, and rise up in obedience to that command in order to be forgiven. If we doubt whether it is possible; if we say, I don't believe Jesus has paid for my sins, therefore, I will not obey his command, or if we say, I can't believe I am really forgiven because after all, I deserve to be unforgiven, since I am so sinful, we cannot experience forgiveness. When we confess that we have sinned and are in need of forgiveness, and repent, Jesus says to us, "Be of good cheer, thy sins are forgiven," and if we accept the word of Christ we are, in that moment, made righteous through Jesus.

The paralytic was healed by the word of Christ. It is the word of Christ that justifies us. The Word of God has this kind of power—the power to accomplish the thing spoken. This is also illustrated in creation: "By the word of the LORD were the heavens made; and all the host of them by the breath of his mouth…For he spake, and it was done; he commanded, and it stood fast."[15] The Word of God has in it the power to do what it says.

The power that healed the paralytic was the same power that forgave him. The power that healed him was the power that maintained his healing. The power of the Word of God that has forgiven us, is the same power that provides victory over sin. If God

---

[14] E. G. White, *The Desire of Ages* (1898), p. 268.1-4.

[15] Psalm 33:6-9

does not have the power to keep us from sinning, he does not have the power to forgive.

"Look unto me, and be ye saved, all the ends of the earth: for I am God, and there is none else. I have sworn by myself, the word is gone out of my mouth in righteousness."[16] The Lord has spoken. He has given to us the promise and "because he could swear by no greater, he sware by himself,"[17] He says, "Surely, shall one say, in the LORD have I righteousness and strength... In the LORD shall all the seed of Israel be justified, and shall glory."[18] He has given us the guaranty that we can be justified in him and thereby attain righteousness, and he is the pledge of surety that makes good on the promise.

---

[16] Isaiah 45:22-23

[17] Hebrews 6:13

[18] Isaiah 45:24-25

4. The Invitation

Throughout scripture time and again the invitation is given: Come, the Lord says, come. He wants you to come unto him now, just as you are. He wants to rescue you from this world of sin and suffering.

"In the last day, that great day of the feast [of Tabernacles], Jesus stood and cried, saying, If any man thirst, let him come unto me, and drink. He that believeth on me, as the scripture hath said, out of his belly shall flow rivers of living water."[1] "The Spirit and the bride say, Come. And let him that heareth say, Come. And let him that is athirst come. And whosoever will, let him take the water of life freely."[2] "Ho, every one that thirsteth, come ye to the waters, and he that hath no money; come ye, buy, and eat; yea, come, buy wine and milk without money and without price. Wherefore do ye spend money for that which is not bread? and your labour for that which satisfieth not? hearken diligently unto me, and eat ye that which is good, and let your soul delight itself in fatness. Incline your ear, and come unto me: hear, and your soul shall live; and I will make an everlasting covenant with you, even the sure mercies of David."[3]

"Not by painful struggles or wearisome toil, not by gift or sacrifice, is righteousness obtained; but it is freely given to every soul who hungers and thirsts to receive it."[4] "And Jesus said unto them, I am the bread of life: he that cometh to me shall never hunger; and he that believeth on me shall never thirst. All that the Father giveth me shall come to me; and him that cometh to me I will in no wise cast out. No man can come to me, except the Father which hath sent me draw him: and I will raise him up at the last day."[5]

"You may come to Jesus in faith, and without delay. His provision is rich and free, his love is abundant, and he will give you grace to wear

---

[1] John 7:37-38

[2] Revelation 22:17

[3] Isaiah 55:13

[4] E. G. White, *Thoughts From the Mount of Blessings* (Mountain View, CA: Pacific Press Publishing Association, 1896), p. 18.2.

[5] John 6:35, 37, 44

his yoke and to lift his burden with cheerfulness. You may claim your right to his blessing by virtue of his promise. You may enter into his kingdom, which is his grace, his love, his righteousness, his peace and joy in the Holy Ghost. If you feel in deepest need, you may be supplied with all his fullness; for Christ says, 'I came not to call the righteous, but sinners to repentance.'

"Christ is calling souls to come unto Him, and it is for our present and eternal interest to hear and respond to the call. Jesus says, 'Ye have not chosen Me, but I have chosen you.' Then let all who would be called children of God respond to the invitation of Christ, and place themselves where the light of heaven will shine upon them, where they will realize what it is to be hearers and doers of the words of Christ, what it is to follow the Light of the world, and be accepted in the Beloved.

"Everything that God could do has been done for the salvation of man. In one rich gift He poured out the treasures of heaven. He invites, He pleads, He urges; but He will not compel men to come unto Him. He waits for their co-operation. He waits for the consent of the will, that He may bestow upon the sinner the riches of his grace, reserved for him from the foundation of the world. A man does not build himself into an habitation for the Spirit, and unless there is a co-operation of man's will with God's will, the Lord can do nothing for him. Though the Lord is the great Master-worker, yet the human agent has his part to act with the divine worker, or the heavenly building cannot be completed. All the power is of God; yet all the responsibility rests with the human agent, for God can do nothing without the co-operation of man. Though weak, erring, frail, sinful, and imperfect, the Lord holds out to man the privilege of co-partnership with Himself."[6]

"'Abide in me,' comes to every soul from the lips of Jesus Christ. Who is He that thus so heartily gives us the invitation? This invitation is genuine. It has no deception in it. His Word is truth. He is the propitiation for not only your sins, but the sins of the whole world. He would have you obey His Word that all His promises may be fulfilled in you. If you come to Him in penitence and repent of your sins, His pardon is full and free. His love is greater than the love of a parent

---

[6] E. G. White, The Messenger, April 26, 1893, par. 1-3.

for his child. He longs to make you a partaker of His blessings, and of the joy of His love, most sweet and precious."[7]

"The sinner is represented as a lost sheep, and a lost sheep never returns to the fold unless he is sought after and brought back to the fold by the shepherd. No man of himself can repent, and make himself worthy of the blessing of justification. The Lord Jesus is constantly seeking to impress the sinner's mind and attract him to behold Himself, the Lamb of God, which taketh away the sins of the world. We cannot take a step toward spiritual life save as Jesus draws and strengthens the soul, and leads us to experience that repentance which needeth not to be repented of."[8]

"The LORD hath appeared of old unto me, saying, Yea, I have loved thee with an everlasting love: therefore with lovingkindness have I drawn thee."[9] "As you come to Him, believe that He accepts you, because He has promised. You can never perish while you do this— never."[10]

"The world's Redeemer endured sufferings commensurate to the guilt of a lost world. The sacrifice of Christ on Calvary's cross fulfilled the demands of the law, and when a sense of sin presses upon the heart, and the burden seems intolerable, Jesus invites the sinner to look to Him and live. There is power in Christ to cleanse the soul. 'Come now, and let us reason together, saith the Lord; though your sins be as scarlet, they shall be as white as snow; though they be red like crimson, they shall be as wool.' [Isaiah 1:18]. The gift of life has been freely, graciously, joyously offered to fallen man. Encircling the throne of God is the rainbow of promise, that God will receive every sinner who gives up all hope of eternal life on the ground of his own righteousness, and accepts the righteousness of the world's Redeemer, believing in Christ as his personal Saviour. It is when the sinner realizes that he is without hope, lost, condemned to eternal death, incapable of doing anything to redeem himself, but accepting

---

[7] E. G. White, *Manuscript 194, 1898*.6

[8] E. G. White, *Selected Messages* (1958), Vol. 1, p. 390.2.

[9] Jeremiah 31:3

[10] E. G. White, *The Ministry of Healing* (Mountain View, CA: Pacific Press Publishing Association, 1905), p. 65.4.

of Christ as his complete Saviour, that the word of God is fulfilled, when He says, 'I will be merciful to their unrighteousness, and their sins and their iniquities will I remember no more.'" [Hebrews 8:12].[11]

All we can ever do toward our salvation is to accept the invitation to come to Christ. It is by faith that we receive Christ's righteousness, but even the faith is not ours: "Knowing that a man is not justified by the works of the law, but by the faith of Jesus Christ, even we have believed in Jesus Christ, that we might be justified by the faith of Christ."[12] We receive Christ's righteousness by the faith of Jesus; not by our faith in Jesus.[13] Have you ever felt that you did not have enough faith? Jesus lived a perfect life; when he gives us his righteousness he also gives us his faith.

"Perfection through our own good works we can never attain. The soul who sees Jesus by faith repudiates his own righteousness. He sees himself as incomplete, his repentance insufficient, his strongest faith but feebleness, his most costly sacrifice as meager, and he sinks in humility at the foot of the cross. But a voice speaks to him from the oracles of God's Word. In amazement he hears the message, 'Ye are complete in him' (Colossians 2:10). Now all is at rest in his soul. No longer must he strive to find some worthiness in himself, some meritorious deed by which to gain the favor of God. "Beholding the Lamb of God, which taketh away the sin of the world, he finds the peace of Christ; for pardon is written against his name, and he accepts the word of God, 'Ye are complete in him.' How hard is it for humanity, long accustomed to cherish doubt, to grasp this great truth! But what peace it brings to the soul, what vital life!"[14]

"Come unto me, all ye that labour and are heavy laden, and I will give you rest. Take my yoke upon you, and learn of me; for I am meek and lowly in heart: and ye shall find rest unto your souls. For my yoke is easy, and my burden is light."[15]

---

[11] E. G. White, *The Messenger,* May 10, 1893, par. 1.

[12] Galatians 2:16

[13] Revelation 14:12

[14] E. G. White, *The Signs of the Times,* July 4, 1892, par. 8-9.

[15] Matthew 11:28-30

5. Righteousness Manifest in Obedience

"The works of his hands are verity and judgment; all his commandments are sure. They stand fast for ever and ever, and are done in truth and uprightness."[1] "A certain ruler asked him, saying, Good Master, what shall I do to inherit eternal life? And Jesus said unto him... Thou knowest the commandments, Do not commit adultery, Do not kill, Do not steal, Do not bear false witness, Honour thy father and thy mother."[2]

"The condition of eternal life is now just what it always has been— just what it was in Paradise before the fall of our first parents— perfect obedience to the law of God, perfect righteousness. If eternal life were granted on any condition short of this, then the happiness of the whole universe would be imperiled. The way would be open for sin, with all its train of woe and misery, to be immortalized."[3] How is it possible to achieve perfect obedience when each of us has already sinned? "All have sinned, and come short of the glory of God,"[4] "there is none righteous, no, not one."[5] At first this seems like bad news, until we realize that God proposes by his spilled blood to pay for our debt of sin and substitute his perfect life for our life of guilt. He has offered you a money order that he has already paid for, so that when you stand before the judgment your debt is paid and his righteousness stands in place of your unrighteousness. "Since we are sinful, unholy, we cannot perfectly obey the holy law. We have no righteousness of our own with which to meet the claims of the law of God. But Christ has made a way of escape for us. He lived on earth amid trials and temptations such as we have to meet. He lived a sinless life. He died for us, and now He offers to take our sins and give us His righteousness. If you give yourself to Him, and accept Him as your Saviour, then, sinful as your life may have been, for His sake you are accounted righteous. Christ's character stands in place

---

[1] Psalm 111:7-8

[2] Luke 18:18, 20

[3] E. G. White, *Steps to Christ* (1892), p. 62.1

[4] Romans 3:23

[5] Romans 3:10

of your character, and you are accepted before God just as if you had not sinned."[6]

"Christ consented to die in the sinner's stead, that man, by a life of obedience, might escape the penalty of the law of God. His death did not make the law of none effect; it did not slay the law, lessen its holy claims, nor detract from its sacred dignity. The death of Christ proclaimed the justice of His Father's law in punishing the transgressor, in that He consented to suffer the penalty of the law Himself in order to save fallen man from its curse. The death of God's beloved Son on the cross shows the immutability of the law of God. His death magnifies the law and makes it honorable, and gives evidence to man of its changeless character. From His own divine lips are heard the words: 'Think not that I am come to destroy the law, or the prophets: I am not come to destroy, but to fulfill.' The death of Christ justified the claims of the law."[7]

"No repentance is genuine that does not work reformation. The righteousness of Christ is not a cloak to cover unconfessed and unforsaken sin; it is a principle of life that transforms the character and controls the conduct. Holiness is wholeness for God; it is the entire surrender of heart and life to the indwelling of the principles of heaven."[8]

"Like the angels, the dwellers in Eden had been placed upon probation; their happy estate could be retained only on condition of fidelity to the Creator's law. They could obey and live, or disobey and perish. God had made them the recipients of rich blessings; but should they disregard His will, He who spared not the angels that sinned, could not spare them; transgression would forfeit His gifts and bring upon them misery and ruin."[9]

"'Abraham believed God, and it was imputed unto him for righteousness: and he was called the friend of God.' James 2:23. And Paul says, 'They which are of faith, the same are the children of

---

[6] E. G. White, *Steps to Christ* (1892), p. 62.2.

[7] E. G. White, *Testimonies for the Church* (1871), Vol. 2, p. 200.2.

[8] E. G. White, *The Desire of Ages* (1898), p. 555.6

[9] E. G. White, *Patriarchs and Prophets* (1890), p. 53.1.

Abraham.' Galatians 3:7. But Abraham's faith was made manifest by his works. 'Was not Abraham our father justified by works, when he had offered Isaac his son upon the altar? Seest thou how faith wrought with his works, and by works was faith made perfect?' James 2:21, 22. There are many who fail to understand the relation of faith and works. They say, 'Only believe in Christ, and you are safe. You have nothing to do with keeping the law.' But genuine faith will be manifest in obedience. Said Christ to the unbelieving Jews, 'If ye were Abraham's children, ye would do the works of Abraham.' John 8:39. And concerning the father of the faithful the Lord declares, 'Abraham obeyed My voice, and kept My charge, My commandments, My statutes, and My laws.' Genesis 26:5. Says the apostle James, 'Faith, if it hath not works, is dead, being alone.' James 2:17. And John, who dwells so fully upon love, tells us, 'This is the love of God, that we keep His commandments.' 1 John 5:3."[10]

"The same law that was engraved upon the tables of stone is written by the Holy Spirit upon the tables of the heart. Instead of going about to establish our own righteousness we accept the righteousness of Christ. His blood atones for our sins. His obedience is accepted for us. Then the heart renewed by the Holy Spirit will bring forth 'the fruits of the Spirit.' Through the grace of Christ we shall live in obedience to the law of God written upon our hearts. Having the Spirit of Christ, we shall walk even as He walked. Through the prophet He declared of Himself, 'I delight to do Thy will, O My God: yea, Thy law is within My heart.' Psalm 40:8. And when among men He said, 'The Father hath not left Me alone; for I do always those things that please Him.' John 8:29.

"The great Teacher came to our world to stand at the head of humanity, to thus elevate and sanctify humanity by His holy obedience to all of God's requirements, showing it is possible to obey all the commandments of God. He has demonstrated that a lifelong obedience is possible. Thus He gives chosen, representative men to the world, as the Father gave the Son, to exemplify in their life the life of Jesus Christ."[11] "'He that hath My commandments, and keepeth them, he it is that loveth Me; and he that loveth Me shall be

---

[10] E. G. White, *Patriarchs and Prophets* (1890), p. 153.4.

[11] E. G. White, *Our Father Cares* (Hagerstown, MD: Review and Herald Publishing Association, 1991), p. 310.4.

loved of My Father, and I will love him, and will manifest Myself to him.' Again Christ repeated the condition of union with Him. This promise is made to every sincere Christian. Our Saviour speaks so plainly that no one need fail to understand that true love will always produce obedience. The religion of Jesus Christ is love. Obedience is the sign of true love. Christ and the Father are one, and those who in truth receive Christ, will love God as the great centre of their adoration, and will also love one another."[12] "Whatever is to be done at His command may be accomplished in His strength. All His biddings are enablings."[13]

"The apostle Paul clearly presents the relation between faith and the law under the new covenant. He says: 'Being justified by faith, we have peace with God through our Lord Jesus Christ.' 'Do we then make void the law through faith? God forbid: yea, we establish the law.' 'For what the law could not do, in that it was weak through the flesh'—it could not justify man, because in his sinful nature he could not keep the law—'God sending His own Son in the likeness of sinful flesh, and for sin, condemned sin in the flesh: that the righteousness of the law might be fulfilled in us, who walk not after the flesh, but after the Spirit.' Romans 5:1; 3:31; 8:3, 4."[14]

"There are two errors against which the children of God—particularly those who have just come to trust in His grace—especially need to guard. The first, already dwelt upon, is that of looking to their own works, trusting to anything they can do, to bring themselves into harmony with God. He who is trying to become holy by his own works in keeping the law, is attempting an impossibility. All that man can do without Christ is polluted with selfishness and sin. It is the grace of Christ alone, through faith, that can make us holy.
"The opposite and no less dangerous error is that belief in Christ releases men from keeping the law of God; that since by faith alone we become partakers of the grace of Christ, our works have nothing to do with our redemption....

---

[12] E. G. White, *The Bible Echo*, June 17, 1901, par. 9.

[13] E. G. White, *Christ's Object Lessons* (Nampa, ID: Pacific Press, 1900), p. 333.1.

[14] E. G. White, *Patriarchs and Prophets* (1890), p. 372.1-373.1.

"We do not earn salvation by our obedience; for salvation is the free gift of God, to be received by faith. But obedience is the fruit of faith."[15]

"The subject of man's personal responsibility is understood by but few; and yet it is a matter of the greatest importance. We may each obey and live, or we may transgress God's law, defy His authority, and receive the punishment that is meet. Then to every soul the question comes home with force, Shall I obey the voice from heaven, the ten words spoken from Sinai,[16] or shall I go with the multitude who trample on that fiery law? To those who love God it will be the highest delight to keep His commandments, and to do those things that are pleasing in His sight. But the natural heart hates the law of God, and wars against its holy claims. Men shut their souls from the divine light, refusing to walk in it as it shines upon them. They sacrifice purity of heart, the favor of God, and their hope of heaven, for selfish gratification or worldly gain.

"Says the psalmist, 'The law of the Lord is perfect' (Psalm 19:7). How wonderful in its simplicity, its comprehensiveness and perfection, is the law of Jehovah! It is so brief that we can easily commit every precept to memory, and yet so far-reaching as to express the whole will of God, and to take cognizance, not only of the outward actions, but of the thoughts and intents, the desires and emotions, of the heart. Human laws cannot do this. They can deal with the outward actions only. A man may be a transgressor, and yet conceal his misdeeds from human eyes; he may be a criminal—a thief, a murderer, or an adulterer—but so long as he is not discovered, the law cannot condemn him as guilty. The law of God takes note of the jealousy, envy, hatred, malignity, revenge, lust, and ambition that surge through the soul, but have not found expression in outward action, because the opportunity, not the will, has been wanting. And these sinful emotions will be brought into the account in the day when 'God shall bring every work into judgment, with every secret thing, whether it be good, or whether it be evil' (Ecclesiastes 12:14)."[17]

---

[15] E. G. White, *Steps to Christ* (1892), p. 59.4-61.1.

[16] Exodus 20:3-17

[17] E. G. White, *Selected Messages* (1958), Vol. 1, p. 216.3-217.1.

Jesus said, "every good tree bringeth forth good fruit; but a corrupt tree bringeth forth evil fruit. A good tree cannot bring forth evil fruit, neither can a corrupt tree bring forth good fruit."[18] Therefore, Scripture declares that all are evil trees: "They are all gone aside, they are all together become filthy: there is none that doeth good, no, not one."[19] If we are corrupt trees, then, by nature, the only thing we can bring forth is evil fruit. In order for a tree to bring forth good fruit, it must first become a good tree: "through the righteousness of Christ we shall stand before God pardoned, and as though we had never sinned."[20] By the acceptance of the obedience of Christ in place of our sinfulness, we are made righteous. Then good fruit is produced automatically, as a result of being made a good tree. Many Christians work very hard to produce good fruit—righteous deeds— without first becoming righteous.

"Whereby are given unto us exceeding great and precious promises: that by these ye might be partakers of the divine nature, having escaped the corruption that is in the world through lust."[21] "Believing in Jesus as his personal Saviour, accepting of his righteousness by faith, the sinner becomes a partaker of the divine nature, and escapes the corruption that is in the world through lust. It is through the indwelling of the Holy Spirit that the Christian is enabled to resist temptation and to work righteousness. Without the divine nature, without the influence of the Spirit of God, man cannot work out his own salvation; for God must work in him to will and to do of his good pleasure. Christ has said, 'Without Me ye can do nothing.'"[22]

"The first step in the path of obedience is to surrender the will to God. This may seem a difficult thing to do; for Satan will present every possible objection, and will manufacture difficulties, and magnify perplexities before the mind; but take the first step, and the next step on the ladder of progress will be easier. This ladder must be climbed round by round; but God is above the ladder, and His glory will illuminate every step of advancement. The path of faith and

---

[18] Matthew 7:17-18

[19] Psalms 14:3

[20] E. G. White, *The Signs of the Times*, April 10, 1893, par. 4.

[21] 2 Peter 1:4

[22] E. G. White, *The Messenger, April 26, 1893, par. 4.*

self-denial is an upward path; its way is heavenward, and as you advance, the misleading clouds of doubt and evil will be left behind."[23]

"But wilt thou know, O vain man, that faith without works is dead? Was not Abraham our father justified by works, when he had offered Isaac his son upon the altar? Seest thou how faith wrought with his works, and by works was faith made perfect? And the scripture was fulfilled which saith, Abraham believed God, and it was imputed unto him for righteousness: and he was called the Friend of God. Ye see then how that by works a man is justified, and not by faith only. Likewise also was not Rahab the harlot justified by works, when she had received the messengers, and had sent them out another way? For as the body without the spirit is dead, so faith without works is dead also."[24]

"In everything that tends to the sustenance of man is seen the concurrence of divine and human effort. There can be no reaping unless the human hand acts its part in the sowing of the seed. But without the agencies which God provides in giving sunshine and showers, dew and clouds, there would be no increase. Thus it is in every business pursuit, in every department of study and science. Thus it is in spiritual things, in the formation of the character, and in every line of Christian work. We have a part to act, but we must have the power of divinity to unite with us, or our efforts will be in vain."[25]

"And hereby we do know that we know him, if we keep his commandments. He that saith, I know him, and keepeth not his commandments, is a liar, and the truth is not in him. But whoso keepeth his word, in him verily is the love of God perfected: hereby know we that we are in him."[26]

---

[23] E. G. White, *The Bible Echo*, April 6, 1903, par. 1.

[24] James 2:20-26

[25] E. G. White, *Christ's Object Lessons* (1900), p. 82.1.

[26] 1 John 2:3-5

6. Many Had Lost Sight of Jesus

As of 2015-2016 47% of Americans cannot even come up with $400 to cover an emergency room visit; 62% of Americans do not have $1,000 in savings; a Canadian poll found half of respondents within $200 of being unable to pay their bills; one in three Americans have not saved a dime for retirement; the number of American men aged 24-55 that are working is lower now than in 1940 at the end of the Great Depression; 51% of working Americans make less than $30,000 per year (with the poverty line for a family of five at $29,000/year), student loan debt is up 10-fold over 20 years; half of all 25 year olds live with their parents[1] and the average American household debt is nearly $300,000.

The typical American views 4.7 hours of television per day, which is 33 hours per week or 142 hours per month. A full time, forty-hour work week averages 172 hours per month. In addition, the average American spends two hours per day on the internet, which is 14 hours per week or 61 hours per month. The average American household has more television sets than family members. The typical American child will spend more time watching television by age six than they will spend with their father in their entire lifetime. The average American youth will rack up 10,000 hours of video games by age 21. Five million Americans are gaming more than 40 hours per week. The time spent on media by the average American Christian is 25:1 compared to the time spent on Bible study, worship and prayer.[2]

"Satan's work is to lead men to ignore God, to so engross and absorb the mind that God will not be in their thoughts. The education they have received has been of a character to confuse the mind, and eclipse the true light. Satan does not wish the people to have a knowledge of God; and if he can set in operation games and theatrical performances that will so confuse the senses of the young that human beings will perish in darkness while light shines all about them, he is well pleased."[3]

---

[1] Scott Ritsema, *Second Beast Rising*, Vol. 1, Disk 8, 55:30.00-1:02:00.00

[2] Scott Ritsema, *Media on the Brain*, Disk 1, 00:06.40-0:11.15

[3] E. G. White, *The Review and Herald,* March 13, 1900, par. 5.

"Satan is delighted when he sees human beings using their physical and mental powers in that which does not educate, which is not useful, which does not help them to be a blessing to those who need their help. While the youth are becoming expert in games that are of no real value to themselves or to others, Satan is playing the game of life for their souls, taking from them the talents that God has given them, and placing in their stead his own evil attributes. It is his effort to lead men to ignore God. He seeks to engross and absorb the mind so completely that God will find no place in the thoughts. He does not wish people to have a knowledge of their Maker, and he is well pleased if he can set in operation games and theatrical performances that will so confuse the senses of the youth that God and heaven will be forgotten."[4]

"And take heed to yourselves, lest at any time your hearts be overcharged with surfeiting, and drunkenness, and cares of this life, and so that day come upon you unawares. For as a snare shall it come on all them that dwell on the face of the whole earth."[5] "And be not conformed to this world: but be ye transformed by the renewing of your mind, that ye may prove what is that good, and acceptable, and perfect, will of God."[6] "But put ye on the Lord Jesus Christ, and make not provision for the flesh, to fulfil the lusts thereof."[7]

"In our association with one another, we should take heed lest we forget Jesus, and pass along unmindful that He is not with us. When we become absorbed in worldly things so that we have no thought for Him in whom our hope of eternal life is centered, we separate ourselves from Jesus and from the heavenly angels. These holy beings cannot remain where the Saviour's presence is not desired, and His absence is not marked. This is why discouragement so often exists among the professed followers of Christ."[8] "If Joseph and Mary had stayed their minds upon God by meditation and prayer, they would have realized the sacredness of their trust, and would not

---

[4] E. G. White, *Councils to Parents, Teachers, and Students* (Mountain View, CA: Pacific Press Publishing Association, 1913), p. 274.3.

[5] Luke 21:34-35

[6] Romans 12:2

[7] John 13:14

[8] E. G. White, *The Desire of Ages* (1898), p. 83.2.

have lost sight of Jesus. By one day's neglect they lost the Saviour; but it cost them three days of anxious search to find Him. So with us; by idle talk, evilspeaking, or neglect of prayer, we may in one day lose the Saviour's presence, and it may take many days of sorrowful search to find Him, and regain the peace that we have lost."[9]

"The Lord would not have any one of us be presumptuous, care not for health, and make no provision whatever for a sustenance; but when He sees the world taking all the thoughts and absorbing all the affections, He sees that eternal realities are lost sight of. He would correct this evil, which is the work of Satan. The mind, which should be trained to high, elevated contemplation of eternal realities, becomes common, bearing the image of the earthly. Jesus comes to present the advantages and beautiful imagery of the heavenly, that the attractions of heaven shall become familiar to the thoughts, and memory's hall be hung with pictures of celestial and eternal loveliness.
"He sees the chambers of the mind filled with those things which defile."[10]

"Christians misrepresent their heavenly Father when they go mourning and groaning, as though they were burdened with an enormous load, when their countenances are expressive of gloom and despondency, and the shadow encompasses their souls. But let them not think they are serving God in so doing; they are doing Satan's work in misrepresenting God and his service. They should go before the Father, and plead with him for a view of his goodness. They have lost sight of Jesus and his love. Let them go to Christ and study his character, for he came to represent the Father. Shall we receive Satan's misrepresentations of our God, and go on in discouragement, lacking peace and joy in the Holy Ghost? Shall we go on mistrusting our heavenly Father's love and doubting his goodness? What greater injury could we do to our children and our friends than to give them such false impressions of Christian life? It was at an infinite cost to the Father that man's salvation was purchased. The Father suffered with the Son to bring salvation within our reach. It is not his will that one soul should perish, but that all

---

[9] E. G. White, *The Desire of Ages* (1898), p. 83.1.

[10] E. G. White, *Our High Calling* (Washington, D.C.: Review and Herald Publishing Association, 1961), p. 286.2.

should come to repentance and receive eternal life. He has done all that it is possible to do to save fallen man. There was no other way by which man could be brought into harmony with his unchangeable law, save by the death of Christ. Christ became our surety, our sacrifice, Saviour, and example, and when all Heaven has been poured out to us in this gift of God, how shall he not with him freely give us all things?

"How much we lose by doubting the love of God! Why do we not come boldly to a throne of grace, and by living faith lay hold of the merits of the blood of a crucified and risen Saviour? This must be an individual work. I cannot be saved by another's faith, nor can another be saved by my faith. Every soul must be saved by his own righteousness. Can we manufacture this righteousness? No. But Jesus has furnished it for us. When the sinner comes to him he takes his load of sin, and gives him his righteousness. The vilest sinner may claim all that was provided in the plan of salvation through the merits of Christ. He may have the attributes of the Saviour. He may go forth to tell of a living Saviour, and to win men to the truth; for he knows what it is to lay hold of Christ by living faith. He has taken the requisite steps in repentance, confession, and restitution, and he can teach others the way of salvation. He can present Christ as one who left his royal throne, who clothed his divinity with humanity that he might save fallen man. He can present him as one who was rich and yet for our sakes became poor, that we through his poverty might be made rich. He can go without the camp, bearing his reproach. He is willing to deny self that others may be saved."[11]

"Even Christians of long experience are often assaulted with the most terrible doubts and waverings.... You must not consider that for these temptations your case is hopeless.... Hope in God, trust in Him, and rest in His promises."[12] "What is the "rest" promised? It is the consciousness that God is true, that He never disappoints the one who comes to Him. His pardon is full and free, and His acceptance means rest to the soul, rest in His love."[13]

---

[11] E. G. White, *The Signs of the Times*, September 2, 1889 par. 7-8.

[12] E. G. White, *Mind, Character and Personality* (Nashville, TN: Southern Publishing Association, 1977), Vol. 2 p. 794.4.

[13] *Ibid.*, p. 803.1.

"When the devil comes with his doubts and unbeliefs, shut the door of your heart. Shut your eyes so that you will not dwell upon his hellish shadow. Lift them up where they can behold the things which are eternal, and you will have strength every hour. The trial of your faith is much more precious than gold.... It makes you valiant to fight the battle of the Lord....
"You cannot afford to let any doubts come into your mind. Do not please the devil enough to tell about the terrible burdens you are carrying. Every time you do it, Satan laughs that his soul can control you and that you have lost sight of Jesus Christ your Redeemer."[14]

"The sacredness has been lost from our labors, and we do not appreciate divine realities as we should, because we have lost sight of Jesus, and fastened our eyes upon humanity. We must awake from our sleep, that Christ may give us life; for we cannot afford to live in a state of stupidity. We must become representatives of our divine Master."[15]

---

[14] E. G. White, *Mind, Character and Personality* (1977), Vol. 2 p. 794.5-6.

[15] E. G. White, *The Review and Herald,* February 23, 1892, par. 8 .

7. His Divinity

"In the beginning was the Word, and the Word was with God, and the Word was God. The same was in the beginning with God. All things were made by him; and without him was not any thing made that was made. In him was life; and the life was the light of men. And the Word was made flesh, and dwelt among us, (and we beheld his glory, the glory as of the only begotten of the Father,) full of grace and truth."[1] Jesus Christ became a man that he might reveal the love of God to human beings. This same Word that was made flesh and dwelt among us was the Creator of the universe. "Now all this was done, that it might be fulfilled which was spoken of the Lord by the prophet, saying, Behold, a virgin shall be with child, and shall bring forth a son, and they shall call his name Emmanuel, which being interpreted is, God with us."[2] "And without controversy great is the mystery of godliness: God was manifest in the flesh, justified in the Spirit, seen of angels, preached unto the Gentiles, believed on in the world, received up into glory."[3] "Far above all principality, and power, and might, and dominion, and every name that is named, not only in this world, but also in that which is to come:"[4] "God, who at sundry times and in divers manners spake in time past unto the fathers by the prophets, Hath in these last days spoken unto us by his Son, whom he hath appointed heir of all things, by whom also he made the worlds; Who being the brightness of his glory, and the express image of his person, and upholding all things by the word of his power, when he had by himself purged our sins, sat down on the right hand of the Majesty on high."[5] "Giving thanks unto the Father... Who hath delivered us from the power of darkness, and hath translated us into the kingdom of his dear Son.... For by him were all things created, that are in heaven, and that are in earth, visible and invisible, whether they be thrones, or dominions, or principalities, or powers: all things were created by him, and for him: And he is before

---

[1] John 1:1-4, 14

[2] Matthew 1:22-23

[3] 1 Timothy 3:16

[4] Ephesians 1:21

[5] Hebrews 1:1-3

all things, and by him all things consist."[6] "Jesus made a surety of a better testament.... Wherefore he is able also to save them to the uttermost that come unto God by him, seeing he ever liveth to make intercession for them. For such an high priest became us, who is holy, harmless, undefiled, separate from sinners, and made higher than the heavens."[7]

Scripture is exceedingly clear on the divine nature of Jesus Christ.[8] Even the most doubtful of his disciples were convinced of his divinity after his resurrection. "And after eight days again his disciples were within, and Thomas with them: then came Jesus, the doors being shut, and stood in the midst, and said, Peace be unto you. Then saith he to Thomas, Reach hither thy finger, and behold my hands; and reach hither thy hand, and thrust it into my side: and be not faithless, but believing. And Thomas answered and said unto him, My Lord and my God."[9]

"Jesus declared, 'I am the resurrection, and the life.' In Christ is life, original, unborrowed, underived. 'He that hath the Son hath life.' 1 John 5:12. The divinity of Christ is the believer's assurance of eternal life. 'He that believeth in Me,' said Jesus, 'though he were dead, yet shall he live: and whosoever liveth and believeth in Me shall never die. Believest thou this?' [John 11:25,26] Christ here looks forward to the time of His second coming. Then the righteous dead shall be raised incorruptible, and the living righteous shall be translated to heaven without seeing death. The miracle which Christ was about to perform, in raising Lazarus from the dead, would represent the resurrection of all the righteous dead. By His word and His works He declared Himself the Author of the resurrection. He who Himself was soon to die upon the cross stood with the keys of death, a conqueror of the grave, and asserted His right and power to give eternal life."[10]

---

[6] Colossians 1:12, 13, 16

[7] Hebrews 7:22, 24-26

[8] Certain corrupted manuscripts systematically remove evidence for the divinity of Jesus. Unfortunately modern bibles are primarily translated from two of the most corrupt manuscripts in existence. For more information on this subject see Martin Klein, *Thou Hast Magnified Thy Word Above All Thy Name.*

[9] John 20:26-28

[10] E. G. White, *The Desire of Ages* (1898), p. 530.3.

Not only is the theme of the divinity of Christ dwelt upon extensively in Scripture, but his eternal nature is also revealed: "But thou, Bethlehem Ephratah, though thou be little among the thousands of Judah, yet out of thee shall he come forth unto me that is to be ruler in Israel; whose goings forth have been from of old, from everlasting."[11] So exalted is the Son of God, so perfectly one with the Father that he is referred to as the Father: "For unto us a child is born, unto us a son is given: and the government shall be upon his shoulder: and his name shall be called Wonderful, Counsellor, The mighty God, The everlasting Father, The Prince of Peace."[12]

"This Saviour was the brightness of His Father's glory and the express image of His person. He possessed divine majesty, perfection, and excellence. He was equal with God. 'It pleased the Father that in Him should all fullness dwell.' 'Who, being in the form of God, thought it not robbery to be equal with God: but made Himself of no reputation, and took upon Him the form of a servant, and was made in the likeness of men: and being found in fashion as a man, He humbled Himself, and became obedient unto death, even the death of the cross.'"[13]

"Christ was one with the Father before the foundation of the world was laid. This is the light shining in a dark place, making it resplendent with divine, original glory.
"Christ is the pre-existent, self-existent Son of God.... In speaking of His pre-existence, Christ carries the mind back through dateless ages. He assures us that there never was a time when He was not in close fellowship with the eternal God....
"His divine life could not be reckoned by human computation. The existence of Christ before His incarnation is not measured by figures.
"Christ was God essentially, and in the highest sense. He was with God from all eternity, God over all, blessed forevermore. The Lord Jesus Christ, the divine Son of God, existed from eternity, a distinct person, yet one with the Father. He was the surpassing glory of heaven. He was the commander of the heavenly intelligences, and the adoring homage of the angels was received by Him as His right.

---

[11] Micah 5:2

[12] Isaiah 9:6

[13] E. G. White, *Testimonies for the Church* (1871), Vol. 2, p. 200.1.

"He was equal with God, infinite and omnipotent.

"But He humbled Himself, and took mortality upon Him. As a member of the human family, He was mortal; but as a God, He was the fountain of life to the world. He could, in His divine person, ever have withstood the advances of death, and refused to come under its dominion; but He voluntarily laid down His life, that in so doing He might give life and bring immortality to light. He bore the sins of the world, and endured the penalty, which rolled like a mountain upon His divine soul. He yielded up His life a sacrifice, that man should not eternally die. He died, not through being compelled to die, but by His own free will.

"And this wonderful mystery, the incarnation of Christ and the atonement that He made, must be declared to every son and daughter of Adam."[14]

"This wonderful problem—how God could be just, and yet the justifier of sinners—is beyond human ken. As we attempt to fathom it, it broadens and deepens beyond our comprehension. When we look with the eye of faith upon the cross of Calvary, and see our sins laid upon the victim hanging in weakness and ignominy there,—when we grasp the fact that this is God, the everlasting Father, the Prince of Peace,—we are led to exclaim, 'Behold, what manner of love the Father hath bestowed upon us!' Christ could at any moment have called legions of angels to his side; he could have swept every sinner from the face of the earth, and created new beings by his power; but God so loved the world, degraded as it was by sin, that 'he gave his only begotten Son, that whosoever believeth on him should not perish, but have everlasting life.'"[15]

Jesus is the creator of the incomprehensible glories of space, the architect of the fathomless complexity of every living creature, the artist of all beauty; Jesus is Jehovah,[16] the God of Abraham; it was Jesus who delivered the children of Israel out of the bondage of Egypt, who descended on Mt. Sinai in flames of glory to deliver the ten-commandments in awful majesty; Jesus, the prince of all creation is the saviour who paid an infinite price for our redemption. "Behold,

---

[14] E. G. White, *The Faith I Live By* (1958), p. 46.2-8.

[15] E. G. White, *The Youth's Instructor,* February 11, 1897 par. 3.

[16] See Jeremiah 23:5-6

the days come, saith the LORD, that I will raise unto David a righteous Branch, and a King shall reign and prosper, and shall execute judgment and justice in the earth. In his days Judah shall be saved, and Israel shall dwell safely: and this is his name whereby he shall be called, THE LORD[17] OUR RIGHTEOUSNESS."[18]

"Nearly two thousand years ago, a voice of mysterious import was heard in heaven, from the throne of God, 'Lo, I come.' 'Sacrifice and offering Thou wouldest not, but a body hast Thou prepared Me.... Lo, I come (in the volume of the Book it is written of Me,) to do Thy will, O God.' Hebrews 10:5-7. In these words is announced the fulfillment of the purpose that had been hidden from eternal ages. Christ was about to visit our world, and to become incarnate. He says, 'A body hast Thou prepared Me.' Had He appeared with the glory that was His with the Father before the world was, we could not have endured the light of His presence. That we might behold it and not be destroyed, the manifestation of His glory was shrouded. His divinity was veiled with humanity,—the invisible glory in the visible human form."[19]

"The nature of Christ was a combination of the divine and the human. Having all the attributes of God, He also represented the excellencies of humanity and showed that all who believe in Christ as their personal Saviour will perfect a character after Christ's likeness and be qualified to become laborers together with God. By precept and example He uplifts those who are depraved, for through the virtues of Jesus Christ he has become the son of God. His life is like Christ's life, his work is like Christ's work, and he will not fail nor be discouraged, because he is vitalized by the Spirit and power of Jesus Christ. Christ is the Son of God in deed and in truth and in love and is the representative of the Father as well as the representative of the human race. His arm brought salvation. He took humanity, was bone of our bone and flesh of our flesh, and submitted to all the temptations wherewith man would be beset. He showed in the great controversy with Satan that He was fully able to remove the stigma and discount the degradation of sin which Satan had placed upon the human family. By taking humanity and combining it with

---

[17] The Hebrew word translated LORD here is Jehovah.

[18] Jeremiah 23:5-6

[19] E. G. White, *The Desire of Ages* (1898), p. 23.1.

divinity, He was able to meet every demand of the law of God, to overcome every objection which Satan had made prominent, as standing in the way of man's obedience to God's commandments."[20]

None in all the universe is more exalted than Jesus: "Wherefore God also hath highly exalted him, and given him a name which is above every name: That at the name of Jesus every knee should bow, of things in heaven, and things in earth, and things under the earth; And that every tongue should confess that Jesus Christ is Lord, to the glory of God the Father."[21]

"Jesus had united with the Father in making the world. Amid the agonizing sufferings of the Son of God, blind and deluded men alone remain unfeeling. The chief priests and elders revile God's dear Son while in His expiring agonies. Yet inanimate nature groans in sympathy with her bleeding, dying Author. The earth trembles. The sun refuses to behold the scene. The heavens gather blackness. Angels have witnessed the scene of suffering until they can look no longer, and hide their faces from the horrid sight. Christ is dying! He is in despair! His Father's approving smile is removed, and angels are not permitted to lighten the gloom of the terrible hour. They can only behold in amazement their loved Commander, the Majesty of heaven, suffering the penalty of man's transgression of the Father's law... Faith and hope trembled in the expiring agonies of Christ because God had removed the assurance He had heretofore given His beloved Son of His approbation and acceptance. The Redeemer of the world then relied upon the evidences which had hitherto strengthened Him, that His Father accepted His labors and was pleased with His work. In His dying agony, as He yields up His precious life, He has by faith alone to trust in Him whom it has ever been His joy to obey. He is not cheered with clear, bright rays of hope on the right hand nor on the left. All is enshrouded in oppressive gloom. Amid the awful darkness which is felt by sympathizing nature, the Redeemer drains the mysterious cup even to its dregs. Denied even bright hope and confidence in the triumph which will be His in the future, He cries with a loud voice: 'Father, into Thy hands I commend My spirit.' He is acquainted with the character of His Father, with His justice, His mercy, and His great love, and in

---

[20] E. G. White, *Letter 11a, 1894*, pp. 7-8. (To Captain Christiansen of the Pitcairn, Jan. 2, 1894.)

[21] Philippians 2:9-11

submission He drops into His hands. Amid the convulsions of nature are heard by the amazed spectators the dying words of the Man of Calvary.

"Nature sympathized with the suffering of its Author. The heaving earth, the rent rocks, proclaimed that it was the Son of God who died. There was a mighty earthquake. The veil of the temple was rent in twain. Terror seized the executioners and spectators as they beheld the sun veiled in darkness, and felt the earth shake beneath them, and saw and heard the rending of the rocks. The mocking and jeering of the chief priests and elders were hushed as Christ commended His spirit into the hands of His Father. The astonished throng began to withdraw and grope their way in the darkness to the city. They smote upon their breasts as they went and in terror, speaking scarcely above a whisper, said among themselves: 'It is an innocent person that has been murdered. What if, indeed, He is, as He asserted, the Son of God?'"[22]

"The world's Redeemer was treated as we deserve to be treated, in order that we might be treated as he deserved to be treated. He came to our world and took our sins upon his own divine soul, that we might receive his imputed righteousness. He was condemned for our sins, in which he had no share, that we might be justified by his righteousness, in which we had no share. The world's Redeemer gave himself for us. Who was he?—The Majesty of heaven, pouring out his blood upon the altar of justice for the sins of guilty man."[23] How does the Majesty of heaven deserve to be treated? He deserves to be placed on the throne of the universe, where he intends to invite us to sit with him, to be treated as the family of the king of all creation. Here is how he intends to treat us: "To him that overcometh will I grant to sit with me in my throne, even as I also overcame, and am set down with my Father in his throne."[24]

---

[22] E. G. White, *Testimonies for the Church* (1871), Vol. 2, p. 209.2-211.1.

[23] E. G. White, *The Review and Herald*, March 21, 1893, par. 6.

[24] Revelation 3:21

8. His Merits

"Through the merits of Christ we have access to the throne of Infinite Power. 'He that spared not His own Son, but delivered Him up for us all, how shall He not with Him also freely give us all things?' Romans 8:32. The Father gave His Spirit without measure to His Son, and we also may partake of its fullness. Jesus says, 'If ye then, being evil, know how to give good gifts unto your children: how much more shall your heavenly Father give the Holy Spirit to them that ask Him?' Luke 11:13. 'If ye shall ask anything in My name, I will do it.' 'Ask, and ye shall receive, that your joy may be full.' John 14:14: 16:24. "While the Christian's life will be characterized by humility, it should not be marked with sadness and self-depreciation. It is the privilege of everyone so to live that God will approve and bless him. It is not the will of our heavenly Father that we should be ever under condemnation and darkness. There is no evidence of true humility in going with the head bowed down and the heart filled with thoughts of self. We may go to Jesus and be cleansed, and stand before the law without shame and remorse. 'There is therefore now no condemnation to them which are in Christ Jesus, who walk not after the flesh, but after the Spirit.' Romans 8:1."[1]

"The merits of Christ elevate and ennoble humanity, and through the name and grace of Christ it is possible for us to overcome the degradation caused by the Fall, and, through the exalted, divine nature of Christ, to be linked to the Infinite. It is dangerous for us to think that by any easy or common effort we may win the eternal reward. Let us consider how much it cost our Saviour in the wilderness of temptation to carry on in our behalf the conflict with the wily, malignant foe. Satan knew that everything depended upon his success or failure in his attempt to overcome Christ with his manifold temptations. Satan knew that the plan of salvation would be carried out to its fulfillment, that his power would be taken away, that his destruction would be certain, if Christ bore the test that Adam failed to endure."[2]

---

[1] E. G. White, *The Great Controversy* (1911), p. 477.1-2.

[2] E. G. White, *The Review and Herald,* February 5, 1895, par. 4

"The fallen race could be restored only through the merit of Him who was equal with God. Though so highly exalted, Christ consented to take upon Him human nature, that He might work in behalf of man, and reconcile to God his disloyal subject. Christ pleads his merit in our behalf. As our substitute and surety, He undertook to combat the powers of darkness in our behalf, and prevailed against the enemy of our souls, presenting to us the cup of salvation. The Prince of Life consented to bear insult and mockery, pain and death. Upon the cross of Calvary He paid redemption's price for a lost world. It was the world that He loved, the one lost sheep that He would bring back to his fold. The cross of Calvary speaks the amazing love of God for the sinner. He valued him at an infinite price, giving his only begotten Son, that whosoever believeth in Him should not perish, but have everlasting life. If the love of God fails to call forth a response from the human heart, if it fails to soften and subdue the soul, we are utterly lost. There is no reserve power through which to influence the sinner. Heaven's richest gift has been freely offered for our acceptance. No greater manifestation of God's love can be given than that which was given on Calvary's cross. If the love of Christ does not melt and subdue the heart, by what means can man be reached? Have you failed to respond to the pleadings of his Spirit? Then no longer fortify your heart in hardness. Open the door of the heart to receive Christ, the best gift of Heaven. Let not cruel unbelief influence you to refuse the heaven-sent guest. Let not Christ say of you, 'Ye will not come unto Me that ye might have life.' With loving entreaties He follows the sinner, pleading, 'Turn ye, turn ye; for why will ye die?'"[3]

"You are the property of Jesus Christ. He has purchased you at an infinite cost to Himself. His you are by creation and by redemption. Although to you your hope of heaven may be at times uncertain, yet you know in whom to trust. Your hope of heaven is found alone in the merits of Jesus Christ. You may now gain a living experience in the things of God. Looking unto Jesus by faith, trusting in His merits, doubts of His love will vanish as dew before the morning sun."[4]

---

[3] E. G. White, *The Messenger,* April 26, 1893, par. 5.

[4] E. G. White, *Testimonies on Sexual Behavior, Adultery, and Divorce* (Silver Spring, MD: Ellen G. White Estate, 1989), p. 48.2.

"'God so loved the world, that he gave his only begotten Son, that whosoever believeth in him should not perish, but have everlasting life.'

"Who can measure the love of God? Angels cannot comprehend it; it is to them a depth of mystery that they cannot fathom. Angels marvel at the divine love manifested for fallen men; but men themselves remain indifferent and unimpressed. Few respond to the love of God. Few appreciate the marvelous love of Christ in his life of suffering, in his death of shame. Behold him humiliated, mocked, sent from Pilate to Herod, and from Herod to Pilate, condemned, crucified, suspended on the cross, a reproach of men, despised of the people. The sentence of condemnation that was merited by guilty man, angels saw fall upon the innocent Son of God, the loved Commander of their hosts. Well might they be astonished at the love that sustained the Sufferer, who died that we might live. Paul writes, 'God forbid that I should glory, save in the cross of our Lord Jesus Christ.' This should be the language of our hearts also. It is in the cross that our hopes of eternal life are centered; and as we look to Calvary, seeing what sin has done, how can we live any longer therein? It was our sin that caused the Son of God to humble himself unto death, even the death of the cross; and in him dwelt the fullness of the Godhead."[5]

"The sacrifice of self to God through the merits of Christ makes you of infinite value, for clothed in the robe of Christ's righteousness you become the sons and daughters of God. Those who.... ask forgiveness in the name of Jesus will receive their request. At the very first expression of penitence Christ presents the humble suppliant's petition before the throne as His own desire in the sinner's behalf. He says, 'I will pray the Father for you.'

"Jesus, our precious Saviour, could not see us exposed to the fatal snares of Satan and forbear making an infinite sacrifice on our behalf. He interposes Himself between Satan and the tempted soul and says, 'Get thee behind me, Satan. Let me come close to this tempted soul.' He pities and loves every humble, trembling suppliant."[6]

---

[5] E. G. White, *The Signs of the Times*, November 24, 1890 par. 1-2.

[6] E. G. White, *That I Might Know Him* (Washington, D.C.: Review and Herald Publishing Association, 1964), p. 77.3-4.

"The sacrifice of Christ on Calvary is an unanswerable argument showing the immutability of the law. Its penalty was felt by the Son of God in behalf of guilty man, that through his merits the sinner might obtain the virtue of his spotless character by faith in his name. The sinner was provided with a second opportunity to keep the law of God in the strength of his Divine Redeemer."[7]

"Could we see all the activity of human instrumentality, as it appears before God, we would see that only the work accomplished by much prayer, which is sanctified by the merit of Christ, will stand the test of the judgment. When the grand review shall take place, then shall ye return and discern between him that serveth God and him that serveth Him not."[8]

"Money cannot buy it, intellect cannot grasp it, power cannot command it; but to all who will accept it, God's glorious grace is freely given. But men may feel their need, and, renouncing all self-dependence, accept salvation as a gift."[9] "Our only safety is in Christ. 'Other foundation can no man lay than that is laid, which is Jesus Christ.' Those who enter Heaven will not scale its walls by their own righteousness, nor will the gates be opened to them for costly offerings of gold and silver; but they will gain an entrance to the many mansions of the Father's house through the merits of the cross of Christ. Jesus is the ladder by which every soul must mount who would climb from earth to Heaven. But there is round after round of painful ascent; for our characters must be brought into harmony with the law of God, and every advance step in this direction requires self-denial."[10]

"We cannot afford to make any mistake where eternal interests are involved. To be indifferent to the claims of God upon us is most ungrateful. We cannot neglect this great salvation and be guiltless. An eternity of bliss has been purchased for every son and daughter of Adam, and all may have a clear title to the immortal inheritance,

[7] E. G. White, *The Signs of the Times,* May 19, 1890 par. 10.

[8] E. G. White, *The Review and Herald,* July 4, 1893.

[9] E. G. White, *God's Amazing Grace* (Washington, D.C.: Review and Herald Publishing Association, 1973), p. 179.2.

[10] E. G. White, *The Signs of the Times,* June 26, 1884, par. 11.

the eternal substance, if they will in probationary time prove their obedience to the commandments of God. All will be tested in this life. If they... by faith lay hold on the merits of Christ and serve God with all their hearts they will have a title to those mansions that Jesus has prepared for all that love Him."[11] "Let not your heart be troubled: ye believe in God, believe also in me. In my Father's house are many mansions: if it were not so, I would have told you. I go to prepare a place for you. And if I go and prepare a place for you, I will come again, and receive you unto myself; that where I am, there ye may be also."[12]

"Oh! how easy for us to forget God, while he never forgets us; he visits us with his mercies every hour. We would feel that it was a calamity indeed to be forgotten of God. But our Redeemer says, 'I will not forget thee. I have graven thee upon the palms of my hands.' Graven his children with the deep prints of the nails driven through those dear hands which he presents to the Father. He says, I will that those who accept my merits be with me where I am, that they may enjoy the mansions which I have prepared for them at an infinite cost; and angelic songs ring through Heaven, Worthy, worthy, worthy is the Lamb that was slain, and hath all power and might and dominion and glory."[13]

---

[11] E. G. White, *That I Might Know Him* (1964), p. 203.3.

[12] John 14:1-3

[13] E. G. White, *The Review and Herald,* February 26, 1880, par. 6 .

9. His Changeless Love

"Christ's love for His children is as strong as it is tender. It is a love stronger than death, for He died for us. It is a love more true than that of a mother for her children. The mother's love may change, but Christ's love is changeless. 'I am persuaded,' Paul says, 'that neither death, nor life, nor angels, nor principalities, nor powers, nor things present, nor things to come, nor height, nor depth, nor any other creature, shall be able to separate us from the love of God, which is in Christ Jesus our Lord' (Romans 8:38, 39).

"In every trial we have strong consolation. Is not our Saviour touched with the feeling of our infirmities? Has He not been tempted in all points like as we are? And has He not invited us to take every trial and perplexity to Him? Then let us not make ourselves miserable over tomorrow's burdens. Bravely and cheerfully carry the burdens of today. Today's trust and faith we must have. But we are not asked to live more than a day at a time. He who gives strength for today will give strength for tomorrow...."[1]

"What love! What amazing condescension! The King of glory proposed to humble Himself to fallen humanity! He would place His feet in Adam's steps. He would take man's fallen nature,[2] and engage to cope with the strong foe who triumphed over Adam. He would overcome Satan, and in thus doing He would open the way for

---

[1] E. G. White, *In Heavenly Places* (1967), p. 269.3-4.

[2] Romans 8:3 "For what the law could not do, in that it was weak through the flesh, God sending his own Son in the likeness of sinful flesh, and for sin, condemned sin in the flesh."

"Christ did not make believe take human nature; He did verily take it. He did in reality possess human nature. 'As the children are partakers of flesh and blood, he also himself likewise took part of the same' (Hebrews 2:14). He was the son of Mary; He was of the seed of David according to human descent. He is declared to be a man, even the Man Christ Jesus. 'This man,' writes Paul, 'was counted worthy of more glory than Moses, inasmuch as he who hath builded the house hath more honour than the house' (Hebrews 3:3)."
E. G. White, *Selected Messages* (1958), Vol. 1, p. 247.1.

"Clad in the vestments of humanity, the Son of God came down to the level of those He wished to save. In Him was no guile or sinfulness; He was ever pure and undefiled; yet He took upon Him our sinful nature. Clothing His divinity with humanity, that He might associate with fallen humanity, He sought to regain for man that which, by disobedience, Adam had lost for himself and for the world. In His own character He displayed to the world the character of God."
E. G. White, *The Review and Herald*, Dec. 15, 1896.

The Most Precious Message

the redemption from the disgrace of Adam's failure and fall, of all
those who would believe on Him."3

"Who is a God like unto thee, that pardoneth iniquity, and passeth by
the transgression of the remnant of his heritage? he retaineth not his
anger for ever, because he delighteth in mercy. He will turn again, he
will have compassion upon us; he will subdue our iniquities; and thou
wilt cast all their sins into the depths of the sea. Thou wilt perform the
truth to Jacob, and the mercy to Abraham, which thou hast sworn
unto our fathers from the days of old."4 "But now thus saith the LORD
that created thee, O Jacob, and he that formed thee, O Israel, Fear
not: for I have redeemed thee, I have called thee by thy name; thou
art mine. When thou passest through the waters, I will be with thee;
and through the rivers, they shall not overflow thee: when thou
walkest through the fire, thou shalt not be burned; neither shall the
flame kindle upon thee. For I am the LORD thy God, the Holy One of
Israel, thy Saviour: I gave Egypt for thy ransom, Ethiopia and Seba
for thee. Since thou wast precious in my sight, thou hast been
honourable, and I have loved thee: therefore will I give men for thee,
and people for thy life."5 "For I am the LORD, I change not; therefore
ye sons of Jacob are not consumed."6 "This I recall to my mind,
therefore have I hope. It is of the LORD's mercies that we are not
consumed, because his compassions fail not. They are new every
morning: great is thy faithfulness. The LORD is my portion, saith my
soul; therefore will I hope in him. The LORD is good unto them that
wait for him, to the soul that seeketh him. It is good that a man
should both hope and quietly wait for the salvation of the LORD."7

"If you call God your Father, you acknowledge yourselves His
children, to be guided by His wisdom and to be obedient in all things,
knowing that His love is changeless. You will accept His plan for your
life. As children of God, you will hold His honor, His character, His
family, His work, as the objects of your highest interest. It will be your
joy to recognize and honor your relation to your Father and to every

3 E. G. White, *God's Amazing Grace* (1973), p. 23.6.

4 Micah 7:18-20

5 Isaiah 43:1-4

6 Malachi 3:6

7 Lamentations 3:21-26

76

member of His family. You will rejoice to do any act, however humble, that will tend to His glory or to the well-being of your kindred."[8]

"Many who profess to be Christians become excited over worldly enterprises, and their interest is awakened for new and exciting amusements, while they are coldhearted, and appear as if frozen, in the cause of God. Here is a theme, poor formalist, which is of sufficient importance to excite you. Eternal interests are here involved. Upon this theme it is sin to be calm and unimpassioned. The scenes of Calvary call for the deepest emotion. Upon this subject you will be excusable if you manifest enthusiasm. That Christ, so excellent, so innocent, should suffer such a painful death, bearing the weight of the sins of the world, our thoughts and imaginations can never fully comprehend. The length, the breadth, the height, the depth, of such amazing love we cannot fathom. The contemplation of the matchless depths of a Saviour's love should fill the mind, touch and melt the soul, refine and elevate the affections, and completely transform the whole character. The language of the apostle is: 'I determined not to know anything among you, save Jesus Christ, and Him crucified.' We also may look toward Calvary and exclaim: 'God forbid that I should glory, save in the cross of our Lord Jesus Christ, by whom the world is crucified unto me, and I unto the world.'"[9]

"Come near... to Christ the Mighty Healer. Jesus' love to us does not come in some wonderful way. This wonderful manner of His love was evidenced at His crucifixion, and the light of His love is reflected in bright beams from the cross of Calvary. Now it remains for us to accept that love, to appropriate the promises of God to ourselves. "Just repose in Jesus. Rest in Him as a tired child rests in the arms of its mother. The Lord pities you. He loves you. The Lord's arms are beneath you. You have not reined yourself up to feel and to hear; but wounded and bruised, just repose trust in God. A compassionate hand is stretched out to bind up your wounds. He will be more precious to your soul than the choicest friend, and all that can be

---

[8] E. G. White, *Daughters of God* (Hagerstown, MD: Review and Herald Publishing Association, 1998), p. 221.2-3.

[9] E. G. White, *Testimonies for the Church* (1871), Vol. 2 p. 212.1-3.

desired is not comparable to Him. Only believe Him; only trust Him. Your friend in affliction—one who knows."[10]

"In all their affliction he was afflicted, and the angel of his presence saved them: in his love and in his pity he redeemed them; and he bare them, and carried them all the days of old."[11] "The LORD hath appeared of old unto me, saying, Yea, I have loved thee with an everlasting love: therefore with lovingkindness have I drawn thee."[12] "I drew them with cords of a man, with bands of love.... I will heal their backsliding, I will love them freely: for mine anger is turned away from him."[13] "The LORD thy God in the midst of thee is mighty; he will save, he will rejoice over thee with joy; he will rest in his love, he will joy over thee with singing."[14]

"I love them that love me; and those that seek me early shall find me."[15] "Love is strong as death... Many waters cannot quench love, neither can the floods drown it: if a man would give all the substance of his house for love, it would utterly be contemned."[16]

"When men and women can more fully comprehend the magnitude of the great sacrifice which was made by the Majesty of heaven in dying in man's stead, then will the plan of salvation be magnified, and reflections of Calvary will awaken tender, sacred, and lively emotions in the Christian's heart. Praises to God and the Lamb will be in their hearts and upon their lips. Pride and self-esteem cannot flourish in the hearts that keep fresh in memory the scenes of Calvary. This world will appear of but little value to those who appreciate the great price of man's redemption, the precious blood of God's dear Son. All the riches of the world are not of sufficient value to redeem one perishing soul. Who can measure the love Christ felt

---

[10] E. G. White, *The Faith I Live By* (1958), p. 65.7.

[11] Isaiah 63:8-9

[12] Jeremiah 31:3

[13] Hosea 11:4; 14:4

[14] Zephaniah 3:17

[15] Proverbs 8:17

[16] Song of Solomon 8:6-7

for a lost world as He hung upon the cross, suffering for the sins of guilty men? This love was immeasurable, infinite.

"Christ has shown that His love was stronger than death. He was accomplishing man's salvation; and although He had the most fearful conflict with the powers of darkness, yet, amid it all, His love grew stronger and stronger. He endured the hiding of His Father's countenance, until He was led to exclaim in the bitterness of His soul: 'My God, My God, why hast Thou forsaken Me?' His arm brought salvation. The price was paid to purchase the redemption of man, when, in the last soul struggle, the blessed words were uttered which seemed to resound through creation: 'It is finished.'

"The heart of God yearns over His earthly children with a love stronger than death. In giving up His Son, He has poured out to us all heaven in one gift.

"Through that gift there comes to us day by day the unfailing flow of Jehovah's goodness. Every flower, with its delicate tints and sweet fragrance, is given for our enjoyment through that one Gift. The sun and moon were made by Him; there is not a star that beautifies the heavens which He did not make. There is not an article of food upon our tables that He has not provided for our sustenance. The superscription of Christ is upon it all. Everything is supplied to man through the one unspeakable Gift, the only-begotten Son of God. He was nailed to the cross that all these bounties might flow to God's workmanship."[17]

"Who shall separate us from the love of Christ? shall tribulation, or distress, or persecution, or famine, or nakedness, or peril, or sword? As it is written, For thy sake we are killed all the day long; we are accounted as sheep for the slaughter. Nay, in all these things we are more than conquerors through him that loved us. For I am persuaded, that neither death, nor life, nor angels, nor principalities, nor powers, nor things present, nor things to come, Nor height, nor depth, nor any other creature, shall be able to separate us from the love of God, which is in Christ Jesus our Lord."[18]

"It is Christ that loves the world with a love that is infinite. He gave His precious life. He was the Only Begotten of the Father. He is risen

---

[17] E. G. White, *The Faith I Live By* (1958), p. 45.2-3.

[18] Romans 5:8; 8:35-39

again from the dead, and is at the right hand of God, making intercession for us. That same Jesus, with His humanity glorified, with no cessation of His love, is our Saviour. He has enjoined upon us to love one another as He has loved us. Will we then cultivate this love? Shall we be like Jesus?"[19]

"It is the love of Christ that makes our heaven. But when we seek to tell of this love, language fails us. We think of His life on earth, of His sacrifice for us; we think of His work in heaven as our advocate, of the mansions He is preparing for those who love Him; and we can but exclaim, 'O the heights and depths of the love of Christ!' As we linger beneath the cross, we gain a faint conception of the love of God, and we say, 'Herein is love, not that we loved God, but that he loved us, and sent his Son to be the propitiation for our sins.' But in our contemplation of Christ, we are only lingering round the edge of a love that is measureless. His love is like a vast ocean, without bottom or shore.
"In all true disciples this love, like sacred fire, burns on the altar of the heart. It was on the earth that the love of God was revealed through Jesus. It is on the earth that His children are to let this love shine out through blameless lives. Thus sinners will be led to the cross, to behold the Lamb of God."[20]

"Let the soul look to Jesus. 'Behold the Lamb of God, which taketh away the sin of the world' (John 1:29). No one will be forced to look to Christ; but the voice of invitation is sounding in yearning entreaty, 'Look and live.' In looking to Christ, we shall see that His love is without a parallel, that He has taken the place of the guilty sinner, and has imputed unto him His spotless righteousness. When the sinner sees his Saviour dying upon the cross under the curse of sin in his stead, beholding His pardoning love, love awakes in his heart. The sinner loves Christ, because Christ has first loved him, and love is the fulfilling of the law. The repenting soul realizes that God 'is faithful and just to forgive us our sins, and to cleanse us from all unrighteousness.' The Spirit of God works in the believer's soul, enabling him to advance from one line of obedience to another,

---

[19] E. G. White, *Testimonies to Ministers and Gospel Workers* (Mountain View, CA: Pacific Press Publishing Association, 1923), p. 157.3.

[20] E. G. White, *Lift Him Up,* p. 248.5-6.

reaching on from strength to greater strength, from grace to grace in Jesus Christ."[21]

"'Behold the Lamb of God, which taketh away the sin of the world.' John 1:29. The light shining from the cross reveals the love of God. His love is drawing us to Himself. If we do not resist this drawing, we shall be led to the foot of the cross in repentance for the sins that have crucified the Saviour. Then the Spirit of God through faith produces a new life in the soul. The thoughts and desires are brought into obedience to the will of Christ. The heart, the mind, are created anew in the image of Him who works in us to subdue all things to Himself. Then the law of God is written in the mind and heart, and we can say with Christ, 'I delight to do Thy will, O my God.' Psalm 40:8."[22]

"The Saviour says, 'Behold, I stand at the door, and knock; if any man hear My voice, and open the door, I will come in to him, and will sup with him, and he with Me.' Revelation 3:20. He is not repulsed by scorn or turned aside by threatening, but continually seeks the lost ones, saying, 'How shall I give thee up?' Hosea 11:8. Although His love is driven back by the stubborn heart, He returns to plead with greater force, 'Behold, I stand at the door, and knock.' The winning power of His love compels souls to come in. And to Christ they say, 'Thy gentleness hath made me great.' Psalm 18:35."[23] "God is fully able to keep us in the world, but not of the world. His love is not uncertain and fluctuating. Ever He watches over His children with a care that is measureless and everlasting."[24]

"If clouds hide the sun from sight, we do not mourn as though it would never appear again. God's dear face of brightness is not always seen; but we are not to despond. It is our duty to trust him in the darkness, knowing that his love is changeless. Then let us put all our powers into our work; let us devote our voice and pen to the service of God, not laboring in our own strength or to please

[21] E. G. White, *Selected Messages* (1958), Vol. 1 p. 374.2.

[22] E. G. White, *The Desire of Ages* (1898), p. 175.5.

[23] E. G. White, *Christ's Object Lessons* (1900), p. 235.2.

[24] E. G. White, *Fundamentals of Christian Education* (Nashville, TN: Southern Publishing Association, 1923), p. 502.1.

ourselves; and we shall see sinners converted, and God will give us a rich reward."[25]

"If we believe in the power of Jesus' name, and present our petitions to God in his name, we shall never be turned away. The Lord says, 'To this man will I look, even to him that is poor and of a contrite spirit, and trembleth at my word.' The psalmist says, 'He will regard the prayer of the destitute, and not despise their prayer.' Our help cometh from God, who holds all things in his own hands. Our peace is in the assurance that his love is exercised toward us. If faith grasps this assurance, we have gained all; if we lose this assurance, all is lost. When we surrender all we have and are to God, and are placed in trying and dangerous positions, coming in contact with Satan, we should remember that we shall have victory in meeting the enemy in the name and power of the Conqueror. Every angel would be commissioned to come to our rescue, when we thus depend upon Christ, rather than that we should be permitted to be overcome. But we need not expect to get the victory without suffering; for Jesus suffered in conquering for us. While we suffer in his name, while we are called upon to deny appetite, and to withdraw ourselves from lovers of pleasure, we should not murmur, but should rather rejoice that we are privileged in a very small degree to be partakers with Christ of the trial, the sacrifice, the self-denial, and the suffering that our Lord endured on our behalf, that we might obtain eternal salvation."[26]

"Christ has instructed us to call God our Father, to regard him as the fountain of affection, the source of the love that has been flowing from century to century through the channel of the human heart. All the pity, compassion, and love that have been manifested in the earth have had their source in God, and, compared to the love that dwells in his heart, are as a fountain to an ocean. His love is perpetually flowing forth to make the weak strong, and to give courage to the wavering.
"When on this earth, Christ did not make God's power and greatness the chief theme of his discourses. He speaks of him oftenest as our Father, and of himself as our Elder Brother. He desires our minds,

[25] E. G. White, *Gospel Workers* (Washington, D.C.: Review and Herald Publishing Association, 1915), p. 456.2.

[26] E. G. White, *Review and Herald,* February 5, 1895 par. 8.

weakened by sin, to be encouraged to grasp the idea that God is love. He seeks to inspire us with confidence, and to lead us to heed the words, 'Let him take hold of my strength, that he may make peace with me; and he shall make peace with me.'"[27] "His love opens a channel into the wounded and bruised soul and becomes a healing balsam to those who sorrow. His love is as a precious link which binds the souls of the finite to the throne of the Infinite, from whom all blessings flow to the needy and distressed; for he comforts all who mourn..."[28]

"The Lord directs every mind that yields to the power of his love, and reveals to it the mystery of godliness. Yield yourself entirely into his keeping; for his love is everlasting and unchangeable. Consecrate your powers to him. The divine influence of his love will diffuse itself through the chambers of your mind; your soul-temple will be cleansed from all selfishness; your heart, filled with all that is pure and lovely, will reveal the mysteries of redeeming love."[29]

"Jesus assures His disciples of God's sympathy for them in their needs and weaknesses. Not a sigh is breathed, not a pain felt, not a grief pierces the soul, but the throb vibrates to the Father's heart."[30]

"Keep your wants, your joys, your sorrows, your cares, and your fears before God. You cannot burden Him; you cannot weary Him. He who numbers the hairs of your head is not indifferent to the wants of His children. 'The Lord is very pitiful, and of tender mercy.' James 5:11. His heart of love is touched by our sorrows and even by our utterances of them. Take to Him everything that perplexes the mind. Nothing is too great for Him to bear, for He holds up worlds, He rules over all the affairs of the universe. Nothing that in any way concerns our peace is too small for Him to notice. There is no chapter in our experience too dark for Him to read; there is no perplexity too difficult for Him to unravel. No calamity can befall the least of His children, no anxiety harass the soul, no joy cheer, no sincere prayer escape the lips, of which our heavenly Father is unobservant, or in which He

---

[27] E. G. White, *The Review and Herald,* January 19, 1911 par. 12-13.

[28] E. G. White, *The Signs of the Times,* August 15, 1895 par. 1.

[29] *Ibid.,* November 19, 1896 par. 12.

[30] E. G. White, *The Desire of Ages* (1898), p. 356.2.

takes no immediate interest. 'He healeth the broken in heart, and bindeth up their wounds.' Psalm 147:3. The relations between God and each soul are as distinct and full as though there were not another soul upon the earth to share His watchcare, not another soul for whom He gave His beloved Son."[31]

"But God, who is rich in mercy, for his great love wherewith he loved us, Even when we were dead in sins, hath quickened us together with Christ, (by grace ye are saved)."[32] "That Christ may dwell in your hearts by faith; that ye, being rooted and grounded in love, May be able to comprehend with all saints what is the breadth, and length, and depth, and height; And to know the love of Christ, which passeth knowledge, that ye might be filled with all the fulness of God."[33]

"Finally, brethren, farewell. Be perfect, be of good comfort, be of one mind, live in peace; and the God of love and peace shall be with you. The grace of the Lord Jesus Christ, and the love of God, and the communion of the Holy Ghost, be with you all. Amen."[34]

---

[31] E. G. White, *Steps to Christ* (1892), p. 100.1.

[32] Ephesians 2:4-5

[33] Ephesians 3:17-19

[34] 2 Corinthians 13:11, 14

10. All Power is Given into His Hands

"God hath spoken once; twice have I heard this; that power belongeth unto God."[1] "Concerning his Son Jesus Christ our Lord, which was made of the seed of David according to the flesh; And declared to be the Son of God with power, according to the spirit of holiness, by the resurrection from the dead."[2] "And Jesus came and spake unto them, saying, All power is given unto me in heaven and in earth."[3]

"For I am not ashamed of the gospel of Christ: for it is the power of God unto salvation to every one that believeth; to the Jew first, and also to the Greek."[4] "He giveth power to the faint; and to them that have no might he increaseth strength."[5] "As many as received him, to them gave he power to become the sons of God, even to them that believe on his name."[6] "For the preaching of the cross is to them that perish foolishness; but unto us which are saved it is the power of God."[7]

"Ah Lord GOD! behold, thou hast made the heaven and the earth by thy great power and stretched out arm, and there is nothing too hard for thee... the Great, the Mighty God, the LORD of hosts, is his name, Great in counsel, and mighty in work: for thine eyes are open upon all the ways of the sons of men: to give every one according to his ways, and according to the fruit of his doings."[8]

"For thou art my lamp, O LORD: and the LORD will lighten my darkness. For by thee I have run through a troop: by my God have I

---

[1] Psalm 62:11

[2] Romans 1:3-4

[3] Matthew 28:18

[4] Romans 1:16

[5] Isaiah 40:29

[6] John 1:12

[7] 1 Corinthians 1:18

[8] Jeremiah 32:17-19

leaped over a wall. As for God, his way is perfect; the word of the
LORD is tried: he is a buckler to all them that trust in him. For who is
God, save the LORD? and who is a rock, save our God? God is my
strength and power: And he maketh my way perfect. He maketh my
feet like hinds' feet: and setteth me upon my high places. He
teacheth my hands to war; so that a bow of steel is broken by mine
arms. Thou hast also given me the shield of thy salvation: and thy
gentleness hath made me great. Thou hast enlarged my steps under
me; so that my feet did not slip."[9]

"Let us be hopeful and courageous. Despondency in God's service is
sinful and unreasonable. He knows our every necessity. He has all
power. He can bestow upon His servants the measure of efficiency
that their need demands."[10] "Do you suppose that after Christ gave
His precious life to redeem the beings He created He would fail to
give them sufficient power to enable them to overcome by the blood
of the Lamb and the word of their testimony? He has power to save
every individual. At the time of His ascension He said, 'All power is
given unto me in heaven and in earth.' For our redemption all power
is given to Him who stood at the head of humanity. For nearly six
weeks the Sinless One fought a battle with the powers of darkness in
the wilderness of temptation, overcoming not on His account, but on
our account, thus making it possible for every son and daughter of
Adam to overcome through the merit of His sinlessness."[11]

"Could one sin have been found in Christ, had He in one particular
yielded to Satan to escape the terrible torture, the enemy of God and
man would have triumphed. Christ bowed His head and died, but He
held fast His faith and His submission to God. 'And I heard a loud
voice saying in heaven, Now is come salvation, and strength, and
the kingdom of our God, and the power of His Christ: for the accuser
of our brethren is cast down, which accused them before our God
day and night.' Revelation 12:10.
"Satan saw that his disguise was torn away. His administration was
laid open before the unfallen angels and before the heavenly
universe. He had revealed himself as a murderer. By shedding the

[9] 2 Samuel 22:29-37

[10] E. G. White, *Testimonies for the Church* (1904), Vol. 8, p. 38.5.

[11] E. G. White, *Sermons and Talks* (Silver Spring, MD: Ellen G. White Estate, 1994), Vol. 2, p. 175.6.

blood of the Son of God, he had uprooted himself from the sympathies of the heavenly beings. Henceforth his work was restricted. Whatever attitude he might assume, he could no longer await the angels as they came from the heavenly courts, and before them accuse Christ's brethren of being clothed with the garments of blackness and the defilement of sin. The last link of sympathy between Satan and the heavenly world was broken.

"Yet Satan was not then destroyed. The angels did not even then understand all that was involved in the great controversy. The principles at stake were to be more fully revealed. And for the sake of man, Satan's existence must be continued. Man as well as angels must see the contrast between the Prince of light and the prince of darkness. He must choose whom he will serve."[12]

"If everyone who claims to be a child of God was 'alive unto God' (Romans 6:11), what a wonderful witness would be given to the people who come to hear the truth. How different the testimony borne would be from the testimony borne in the formal, dead churches. We are to be filled with faith and life and light. We are to realize that upon every believer rests the great and solemn responsibility of bearing witness to the precious advantages obtained through a belief of the truth. When from every believer the light shines forth in clear, distinct rays, people will realize that the truth we believe has a solemn, sacred power."[13]

"Accompanied by the power of persuasion, the power of prayer, the power of the love of God, the evangelist's work will not, can not, be without fruit. Think of the interest that the Father and the Son have in this work. As the Father loves the Son, so the Son loves those that are his—those who work as he worked to saved perishing souls. None need feel that they are powerless: for Christ declares, 'All power is given unto me in heaven and in earth.' He has promised that he will give this power to his workers. His power is to become their power. They are to link their souls with God. Christ desires all to enjoy the wealth of his grace, which is beyond all computation. It is limitless, exhaustless. It is ours by eternal covenant, if we will be

---

[12] E. G. White, *The Desire of Ages* (1898), p. 761.1-3.

[13] E. G. White, *Letter 31-1900*.10.

workers together with God. It is ours if we will unite with him to bring many sons and daughters to God."[14]

It is in working actively to supply the necessities of the cause of God that we bring our souls in touch with the Source of all power."[15]

"Courage, energy, and perseverance they must possess. Though apparent impossibilities obstruct their way, by His grace they are to go forward. Instead of deploring difficulties, they are called upon to surmount them. They are to despair of nothing, and to hope for everything. With the golden chain of His matchless love, Christ had bound them to the throne of God. It is His purpose that the highest influence in the universe, emanating from the Source of all power, shall be theirs. They are to have power to resist evil, power that neither earth, nor death, nor hell can master, power that will enable them to overcome as Christ overcame."[16]

"Oh, it was poverty indeed apportioned to the Son of God that He should be moving upon a province of His own empire and yet not be recognized or confessed by the nation He came to bless and to save. It was poverty that when He walked among men, scattering blessing as He trod, the anthem of praise floated not around Him, but the air was often freighted with curses and blasphemy. It was poverty that as He passed to and fro among the subjects He came to save, scarcely a solitary voice called Him blessed, scarcely a solitary hand was stretched out in friendship, and scarcely a solitary roof proffered Him shelter. Then look beneath the disguise, and whom do we see? —Divinity, the Eternal Son of God, just as mighty, just as infinitely gifted with all the resources of power, and He was found in fashion as a man."[17]

"These words spake Jesus, and lifted up his eyes to heaven, and said, Father, the hour is come; glorify thy Son, that thy Son also may glorify thee: As thou hast given him power over all flesh, that he should give eternal life to as many as thou hast given him. And this is life eternal, that they might know thee the only true God, and Jesus

---

[14] E. G. White, *The Colporteur Evangelist* (Mountain View, CA: Pacific Press Publishing Association, 1920), p. 33.3.

[15] E. G. White, *Christian Service* (Hagerstown, MD: Review and Herald Publishing Association, 1925), p. 170.3.

[16] *Ibid.*, p. 235.2.

[17] E. G. White, *Manuscript Releases* (1990), Vol. 15 p. 25.3.

Christ, whom thou hast sent."[18] "Behold, I give unto you power to tread on serpents and scorpions, and over all the power of the enemy: and nothing shall by any means hurt you."[19]

"Standing but a step from His heavenly throne, Christ gave the commission to His disciples. "All power is given unto Me in heaven and in earth," He said. "Go ye therefore, and teach all nations." "Go ye into all the world, and preach the gospel to every creature." Mark 16:15. Again and again the words were repeated, that the disciples might grasp their significance. Upon all the inhabitants of the earth, high and low, rich and poor, was the light of heaven to shine in clear, strong rays. The disciples were to be colaborers with their Redeemer in the work of saving the world."[20]

"We give thee thanks, O Lord God Almighty, which art, and wast, and art to come; because thou hast taken to thee thy great power, and hast reigned."[21] "To the only wise God our Saviour, be glory and majesty, dominion and power, both now and for ever. Amen."[22]

---

[18] John 17:1-3

[19] Luke 10:19

[20] E. G. White, *The Desire of Ages* (1898), p. 818.1.

[21] Revelation 11:17

[22] Jude 1:25

11. The Priceless Gift of His Own Righteousness

"By rebellion and apostasy man forfeited the favor of God; not his rights, for he could have no value except as it was invested in God's dear Son. This point must be understood. He forfeited those privileges which God in His mercy presented him as a free gift, a treasure in trust to be used to advance His cause and His glory, to benefit the beings He had made. The moment the workmanship of God refused obedience to the laws of God's kingdom, that moment he became disloyal to the government of God and he made himself entirely unworthy of all the blessings wherewith God had favored him.

"This was the position of the human race after man divorced himself from God by transgression. Then he was no longer entitled to a breath of air, a ray of sunshine, or a particle of food. And the reason why man was not annihilated was because God so loved him that He made the gift of His dear Son that He should suffer the penalty of his transgression. Christ proposed to become man's surety and substitute, that man, through matchless grace, should have another trial—a second probation—having the experience of Adam and Eve as a warning not to transgress God's law as they did. And inasmuch as man enjoys the blessings of God in the gift of the sunshine and the gift of food, there must be on the part of man a bowing before God in thankful acknowledgment that all things come of God. Whatever is rendered back to Him is only His own who has given it."[1]

Through sin and rebellion humanity forfeited all privileges from God, yet even sin would not cause God to withdraw the rights he bestowed on the intelligent beings he had created. "We hold these truths to be self-evident, that all men are created equal, that they are endowed by their Creator with certain unalienable Rights, that among these are Life, Liberty and the pursuit of Happiness."[2] The rights God will never violate include the rights that have been historically held dear in America: freedom of choice, the rights of freedom of conscience, the right to religious liberty, the right to bear arms, the rights to freedom of speech, the right to privacy, the right to redress grievances, and the right to a fair trial.

---

[1] E. G. White, *Faith and Works* (1979), p. 21.1-2.

[2] United States of America, *Declaration of Independence*.

The sacrifice of Christ provides the life and sustenance for every person ever born to freely choose by whom they will be governed. Because of the sacrifice of Christ, God provides the resources needed for the atheist to deny the Creator's existence, for the infidel to speak his blasphemies, for the skeptic to fight against God himself. "He maketh his sun to rise on the evil and on the good, and sendeth rain on the just and on the unjust."[3] His plea that his people fight not against him is proof that such a choice is an option—the right to bear arms, even against God. "O children of Israel, fight ye not against the LORD God of your fathers; for ye shall not prosper."[4]

"To the death of Christ we owe even this earthly life. The bread we eat is the purchase of His broken body. The water we drink is bought by His spilled blood. Never one, saint or sinner, eats his daily food, but he is nourished by the body and the blood of Christ. The cross of Calvary is stamped on every loaf. It is reflected in every water spring."[5]

God himself respects your right to privacy: "Behold, I stand at the door, and knock: if any man hear my voice, and open the door, I will come in to him, and will sup with him, and he with me."[6]

God invites us to redress our grievances with him: "The government of God is not, as Satan would make it appear, founded upon a blind submission, an unreasoning control. It appeals to the intellect and the conscience. 'Come now, and let us reason together' is the Creator's invitation to the beings He has made. Isaiah 1:18. God does not force the will of His creatures. He cannot accept an homage that is not willingly and intelligently given."[7] Job cried, "Oh that I knew where I might find him! that I might come even to his seat! I would order my cause before him, and fill my mouth with arguments. I

---

[3] Matthew 5:45

[4] 2 Chronicles 13:12

[5] E. G. White, *The Desire of Ages* (1898), p. 660.3.

[6] Revelation 3:20

[7] E. G. White, *Steps to Christ* (1892), p. 43.4.

would know the words which he would answer me, and understand what he would say unto me."[8]

Whether we choose to accept the gift of Jesus or crusade against Christ, we retain the right to a fair trial. "For we must all appear before the judgment seat of Christ; that every one may receive the things done in his body, according to that he hath done, whether it be good or bad."[9] "As the features of the countenance are reproduced with marvelous exactness in the camera of the artist, so is the character faithfully delineated in the books above. If Christians were as solicitous to stand faultless in the heavenly records as they are to be represented without a blemish in the picture, how different would their life-history appear.

"Could the vail which separates the visible from the invisible world be swept back, and the children of men behold an angel recording every word and deed to meet them again in the Judgment, how many words that are daily uttered would remain unspoken; how many deeds would remain undone. When all the details of life appear in the books that never contain a false entry, many will find too late that the record testifies against them. There their hidden selfishness stands revealed. There is the record of unfulfilled duties to their fellow-men, of forgetfulness of the Saviour's claims. There they will see how often were given to Satan the time, thought, and strength that belonged to Christ. Sad is the record which angels bear to Heaven. Intelligent beings, professed followers of Christ, are absorbed in the acquirement of worldly possessions or the enjoyment of earthly pleasures. Money, time, and strength are sacrificed for display and self-indulgence; but few are the moments devoted to prayer, to the searching of the Scriptures, to humiliation of soul and confession of sin."[10]

"For thus saith the LORD, Ye have sold yourselves for nought; and ye shall be redeemed without money."[11] "Forasmuch as ye know that ye were not redeemed with corruptible things, as silver and gold, from your vain conversation received by tradition from your fathers;

---

[8] Job 23:3-5

[9] 2 Corinthians 5:10

[10] E. G. White, *The Spirit of Prophecy* (1884), Vol. 4, p. 311.3-312.1.

[11] Isaiah 52:3

But with the precious blood of Christ, as of a lamb without blemish and without spot."[12] "For we have not an high priest which cannot be touched with the feeling of our infirmities; but was in all points tempted like as we are, yet without sin."[13] "Point after point Paul lingered over, in order that those who should read his epistle might fully comprehend the wonderful condescension of the Saviour in their behalf. Presenting Christ as He was when equal with God and with Him receiving the homage of the angels, the apostle traced His course until He had reached the lowest depths of humiliation. Paul was convinced that if they could be brought to comprehend the amazing sacrifice made by the Majesty of heaven, all selfishness would be banished from their lives. He showed how the Son of God had laid aside His glory, voluntarily subjecting Himself to the conditions of human nature, and then had humbled Himself as a servant, becoming obedient unto death, 'even the death of the cross' (Philippians 2:8), that He might lift fallen man from degradation to hope and joy and heaven."[14] "For he hath made him to be sin for us, who knew no sin; that we might be made the righteousness of God in him."[15]

"Unto me, who am less than the least of all saints, is this grace given, that I should preach among the Gentiles the unsearchable riches of Christ; And to make all men see what is the fellowship of the mystery, which from the beginning of the world hath been hid in God, who created all things by Jesus Christ."[16] "To whom God would make known what is the riches of the glory of this mystery among the Gentiles; which is Christ in you, the hope of glory."[17]

"True religion is nothing short of conformity to the will of God, and obedience to all things that he has commanded; and in return, it gives us spiritual life, imputes to us the righteousness of Christ, and

---

[12] 1 Peter 1:18-19

[13] Hebrews 4:15

[14] E. G. White, *The Acts of the Apostles* (Mountain View, CA: Pacific Press Publishing Association, 1911), p. 333.1.

[15] 2 Corinthians 5:21

[16] Ephesians 3:8-9

[17] Colossians 1:27

promotes the healthful and happy exercise of the best faculties of the mind and heart. Infinite riches, the glory and blessedness of eternal life, are bestowed upon us on conditions so simple as to bring the priceless gift within the reach of the poorest and most sinful. We have only to obey and believe. And his commandments are not grievous; obedience to his requirements is essential to our happiness even in this life."[18]

"As it was in the days of Christ, so it is now; the Pharisees do not know their spiritual destitution. To them comes the message, 'Because thou sayest, I am rich, and increased with goods, and have need of nothing; and knowest not that thou art wretched, and miserable, and poor, and blind, and naked: I counsel thee to buy of Me gold tried in the fire, that thou mayest be rich; and white raiment, that thou mayest be clothed, and that the shame of thy nakedness do not appear.' Revelation 3:17, 18. Faith and love are the gold tried in the fire. But with many the gold has become dim, and the rich treasure has been lost. The righteousness of Christ is to them as a robe unworn, a fountain untouched. To them it is said, 'I have somewhat against thee, because thou hast left thy first love. Remember therefore from whence thou art fallen, and repent, and do the first works; or else I will come unto thee quickly, and will remove thy candlestick out of his place, except thou repent.' Revelation 2:4, 5."[19]

"Satan's dominion was that wrested from Adam, but Adam was the vicegerent of the Creator. His was not an independent rule. The earth is God's, and He has committed all things to His Son. Adam was to reign subject to Christ. When Adam betrayed his sovereignty into Satan's hands, Christ still remained the rightful King. Satan can exercise his usurped authority only as God permits."[20] "Adam's sin plunged the race into hopeless misery; but by the sacrifice of the Son of God, a second probation was granted to man. In the plan of redemption a way of escape is provided for all who will avail themselves of it. God knew that it was impossible for man to overcome in his own strength, and he has provided help for him.

---

[18] E. G. White, *Selected Messages* (1980), Vol. 3, 150.4.

[19] E. G. White, *Manuscript Releases* (1990), Vol. 18, p. 202.2.

[20] E. G. White, *The Desire of Ages* (1898), p. 129.4.

How thankful we should be that a way is open for us, by which we can have access to the Father; that the gates are left ajar, so that beams of light from the glory within may shine upon those who will receive them!

"We can understand the value of the human soul only as we realize the greatness of the sacrifice made for its redemption. The word of God declares that we are not our own, that we are bought with a price. It is at an immense cost that we have been placed upon vantage ground, where we can find liberty from the bondage of sin wrought by the fall in Eden."[21]

"All power is given into the hands of Christ, in order that he may dispense rich blessings to men, and impart to them the priceless gifts of his own righteousness. But many, blinded by sin, have lost sight of Christ, and are groping in the dark shadows of discouragement. Go to them with a heart filled with love and tenderness, and tell them of the uplifted Saviour, who is the sacrifice for the whole world; invite them to receive the righteousness of Christ, to claim justification through faith in the divine surety; direct them to the all sufficient atonement made for their sins, to Christ's merits, and his changeless love for the human family."[22]

"Let pride be crucified, and the soul be clad with the priceless robe of Christ's righteousness... It will be to your soul even as the gate of heaven."[23]

"Now unto him that is able to keep you from falling, and to present you faultless before the presence of his glory with exceeding joy, To the only wise God our Saviour, be glory and majesty, dominion and power, both now and for ever. Amen."[24]

---

[21] E. G. White, *Christian Temperance and Bible Hygiene* (Battle Creek, MI: Good Health Publishing Co., 1890), p. 15.3 .

[22] E. G. White, *The Review and Herald,* September 29, 1896, par. 11.

[23] E. G. White, *The Review and Herald,* June 6, 1912, Art. A, par. 6.

[24] Jude 1:24-25

12. The Helplessness of the Human Agent

"Nothing can be more helpless, nothing can be more dependent, than the soul that feels its nothingness, and relies wholly upon the merits of the blood of a crucified and risen Saviour."[1] "There is not a point that needs to be dwelt upon more earnestly, repeated more frequently, or established more firmly in the minds of all, than the impossibility of fallen man meriting anything by his own best good works. Salvation is through faith in Jesus Christ alone."[2]

Even repentance is a result of the drawing of Christ upon the heart. "When before the high priests and Sadducees, Peter clearly presented the fact that repentance is the gift of God. Speaking of Christ, he said, 'Him hath God exalted with his right hand to be a Prince and a Saviour, for to give repentance to Israel, and forgiveness of sins' (Acts 5:31). Repentance is no less the gift of God than are pardon and justification, and it cannot be experienced except as it is given to the soul by Christ. If we are drawn to Christ, it is through His power and virtue. The grace of contrition comes through Him, and from Him comes justification."[3]

"What is justification by faith? It is the work of God in laying the glory of man in the dust, and doing for man that which it is not in his power to do for himself. When men see their own nothingness, they are prepared to be clothed with the righteousness of Christ."[4]

Human beings are helpless without the power of Christ. Any action for good or tendency to right, even in the unbelieving sinner, is as a result of the promptings of the Holy Spirit.

"Wherever there is an impulse of love and sympathy, wherever the heart reaches out to bless and uplift others, there is revealed the working of God's Holy Spirit. In the depths of heathenism, men who have had no knowledge of the written law of God, who have never

---

[1] E. G. White, *The Review and Herald*, February 5, 1895, par. 9.

[2] E. G. White, *The Ellen G. White 1888 Materials* (1987), p. 811.2.

[3] E. G. White, *Selected Messages*, Vol. 1 (1958), p. 389.2-391.1.

[4] E. G. White, *The Faith I Live By* (1958), p. 111.2.

even heard the name of Christ, have been kind to His servants, protecting them at the risk of their own lives. Their acts show the working of a divine power. The Holy Spirit has implanted the grace of Christ in the heart of the savage, quickening his sympathies contrary to his nature, contrary to his education. The "Light which lighteth every man that cometh into the world" (John 1:9), is shining in his soul; and this light, if heeded, will guide his feet to the kingdom of God."[5]

"Many are confused as to what constitutes the first steps in the work of salvation. Repentance is thought to be a work the sinner must do for himself in order that he may come to Christ. They think that the sinner must procure for himself a fitness in order to obtain the blessing of God's grace. But while it is true that repentance must precede forgiveness, for it is only the broken and contrite heart that is acceptable to God, yet the sinner cannot bring himself to repentance, or prepare himself to come to Christ. Except the sinner repent, he cannot be forgiven; but the question to be decided is as to whether repentance is the work of the sinner or the gift of Christ. Must the sinner wait until he is filled with remorse for his sin before he can come to Christ? The very first step to Christ is taken through the drawing of the Spirit of God; as man responds to this drawing, he advances toward Christ in order that he may repent.
"When Satan tells you that you are a sinner, and cannot hope to receive blessing from God, tell him that Christ came into the world to save sinners. We have nothing to recommend us to God; but the plea that we may urge now and ever is our utterly helpless condition that makes His redeeming power a necessity. Renouncing all self-dependence, we may look to the cross of Calvary and say,—

> 'In my hand no price I bring;
> Simply to Thy cross I cling.'"[6]

"Satan may whisper, 'You are too great a sinner for Christ to save.' While you acknowledge that you are indeed sinful and unworthy, you may meet the tempter with the cry, 'By virtue of the atonement, I claim Christ as my Saviour. I trust not to my own merits, but to the precious blood of Jesus, which cleanses me. This moment I hang my helpless soul on Christ.' The Christian life must be a life of constant,

---

[5] E. G. White, *Christ's Object Lessons* (1900), p. 385.1.

[6] E. G. White, *The Desire of Ages* (1898), p. 317.1.

living faith. An unyielding trust, a firm reliance upon Christ, will bring peace and assurance to the soul.

"Be not discouraged because your heart seems hard. Every obstacle, every internal foe, only increases your need of Christ. He came to take away the heart of stone, and give you a heart of flesh. Look to him for special grace to overcome your peculiar faults. When assailed by temptation, steadfastly resist the evil promptings; say to your soul, 'How can I dishonor my Redeemer? I have given myself to Christ; I cannot do the works of Satan.' Cry to the dear Saviour for help to sacrifice every idol, and to put away every darling sin. Let the eye of faith see Jesus standing before the Father's throne, presenting his wounded hands as he pleads for you. Believe that strength comes to you through your precious Saviour."[7]

"When the Lamb of God was crucified on Calvary, the death knell of Satan was sounded; and if the enemy of truth and righteousness can obliterate from the mind the thought that it is necessary to depend upon the righteousness of Christ for salvation, he will do it. If Satan can succeed in leading man to place value upon his own works as works of merit and righteousness, he knows that he can overcome him by his temptations, and make him his victim and prey. Lift up Jesus before the people. Strike the door-posts with the blood of Calvary's Lamb, and you are safe."[8]

In Isaiah chapter 6 the prophet saw a vision of the Almighty, "Beholding the glory of the Son of God caused the prophet himself to appear very insignificant. He felt nothing but contempt for himself. 'I abhor myself! Woe is me, for I am undone.' The more closely we view the Lord Jesus in his purity and loveliness, the less will we esteem self, the less will we strive for the mastery, or even for recognition. When the light of Jesus reveals the deformity of our souls, there will be no desire to lift up ourselves unto vanity. The appearance of self is most unpleasing. The more continuously the sinful man looks upon Jesus, the less he sees in himself to admire, and his soul is prostrated before God in contrition."[9]

---

[7] E. G. White, *The Review and Herald*, May 3, 1881, par. 5-6.

[8] *Ibid.*, September, 3, 1889 par. 20.

[9] *Ibid.*, February 18, 1896 par. 1-3.

"Let no one take the limited, narrow position that any of the works of man can help in the least possible way to liquidate the debt of his transgression. This is a fatal deception. If you would understand it, you must cease haggling over your pet ideas, and with humble hearts survey the atonement. This matter is so dimly comprehended that thousands upon thousands claiming to be sons of God are children of the wicked one, because they will depend on their own works. God always demanded good works, the law demands it, but because man placed himself in sin where his good works were valueless, Jesus' righteousness alone can avail. Christ is able to save to the uttermost because He ever liveth to make intercession for us. All that man can possibly do toward his own salvation is to accept the invitation, 'Whosoever will, let him take the water of life freely' (Revelation 22:17)."[10] "Perfection through our own good works we can never attain. The soul who sees Jesus by faith repudiates his own righteousness. He sees himself as incomplete, his repentance insufficient, his strongest faith but feebleness, his most costly sacrifice as meager, and he sinks in humility at the foot of the cross. But a voice speaks to him from the oracles of God's Word. In amazement he hears the message, 'Ye are complete in him' (Colossians 2:10). Now all is at rest in his soul. No longer must he strive to find some worthiness in himself, some meritorious deed by which to gain the favor of God."[11]

Jesus said of the Pharisees, "Woe unto you, scribes and Pharisees, hypocrites! for ye are like unto whited sepulchres, which indeed appear beautiful outward, but are within full of dead [men's] bones, and of all uncleanness. Even so ye also outwardly appear righteous unto men, but within ye are full of hypocrisy and iniquity."[12] The Pharisees appeared to be righteous on the outside, but did not keep the law. Jesus said, "For I say unto you, That except your righteousness shall exceed the righteousness of the scribes and Pharisees, ye shall in no case enter into the kingdom of heaven."[13]

---

[10] E. G. White, *Selected Messages* (1958), Vol. 1, p. 343.3.

[11] E. G. White, *Reflecting Christ* (Hagerstown, MD: Review and Herald Publishing Association, 1985), p. 76.5.

[12] Matthew 23:27-28

[13] Matthew 5:20

And to the Pharisees he said, "none of you keepeth the law."[14] The unbelieving Jews never attained to the righteous requirements of the law, because they refused the only one who could make them righteous before God. "They being ignorant of God's righteousness, and going about to establish their own righteousness, have not submitted themselves unto the righteousness of God."[15]

"Man cannot possibly meet the demands of the law of God in human strength alone. His offerings, his works, will all be tainted with sin. A remedy has been provided in the Saviour, who can give to man the virtue of his merit, and make him co-laborer in the great work of salvation. Christ is righteousness, sanctification, and redemption to those who believe in him, and who follow in his steps."[16] "Our condition is helpless and hopeless unless infinite mercy is granted us daily, and pardon is written against our names in the heavenly records. Those only who see and feel their spiritual necessities will go to Jesus for that help which they so much need, and which he only can give. He alone can cleanse us from all sin. He alone can place upon us the robe of righteousness."[17]

"It was possible for Adam, before the fall, to form a righteous character by obedience to God's law. But he failed to do this, and because of his sin our natures are fallen, and we cannot make ourselves righteous. Since we are sinful, unholy, we cannot perfectly obey a holy law. We have no righteousness of our own with which to meet the claims of the law of God. But Christ has made a way of escape for us. He lived on earth amid trials and temptations such as we have to meet. He lived a sinless life. He died for us, and now he offers to take our sins and give us his righteousness. If you give yourself to him, and accept him as your Saviour, then, sinful as your life may have been, for his sake you are accounted righteous. Christ's character stands in place of your character, and you are accepted before God just as if you had not sinned."[18]

---

[14] John 7:19

[15] Romans 10:3

[16] E. G. White, *The Review and Herald,* February 4, 1890, par. 4.

[17] E. G. White, *The Signs of the Times,* January 4, 1883, par. 12.

[18] *Ibid.,* November 11, 1915 par. 2.

The Testimony of the faithful and true Witness is, "I know thy works, that thou art neither cold nor hot... thou art lukewarm.... Because thou sayest, I am rich, and increased with goods, and have need of nothing; and knowest not that thou art wretched, and miserable, and poor, and blind, and naked."[19] "Wherefore let him that thinketh he standeth take heed lest he fall."[20] This is our condition; we think we have need of nothing. We think we are good enough. "The True Witness has said, 'Buy of me gold tried in the fire, that thou mayest be rich; and white raiment, that thou mayest be clothed, and that the shame of thy nakedness do not appear.' What is the shame of this nakedness and poverty? It is the shame of clothing ourselves with self-righteousness, and of separating ourselves from God, when he has made ample provision for all to receive his blessing."[21]

"I ask, How can I present this matter as it is? The Lord Jesus imparts all the powers, all the grace, all the penitence, all the inclination, all the pardon of sins, in presenting His righteousness for man to grasp by living faith—which is also the gift of God. If you would gather together everything that is good and holy and noble and lovely in man and then present the subject to the angels of God as acting a part in the salvation of the human soul or in merit, the proposition would be rejected as treason. Standing in the presence of their Creator and looking upon the unsurpassed glory which enshrouds His person, they are looking upon the Lamb of God given from the foundation of the world to a life of humiliation, to be rejected of sinful men, to be despised, to be crucified. Who can measure the infinity of the sacrifice! "[22]

"Encircling the throne of God is the rainbow of promise, that God will receive every sinner who gives up all hope of eternal life on the ground of his own righteousness, and accepts the righteousness of the world's Redeemer, believing in Christ as his personal Saviour. It is when the sinner realizes that he is without hope, lost, condemned to eternal death, incapable of doing anything to redeem himself, but accepting of Christ as his complete Saviour, that the word of God is

---

[19] Revelation 3:15-17

[20] 1 Corinthians 10:12

[21] E. G. White, *Historical Sketches* (1886), p. 139.3.

[22] E. G. White, *Faith and Works* (1979), p. 24.1.

fulfilled, when He says, 'I will be merciful to their unrighteousness, and their sins and their iniquities will I remember no more.'"[23]

"As Christ in His humanity sought strength from His Father, that He might be enabled to endure trial and temptation, so are we to do. We are to follow the example of the sinless Son of God. Daily we need help and grace and power from the Source of all power. We are to cast our helpless souls upon the One who is ready to help us in every time of need. Too often we forget the Lord. Self gives way to impulse, and we lose the victories that we should gain.

"If we are overcome let us not delay to repent, and to accept the pardon that will place us on vantage ground. If we repent and believe, the cleansing power from God will be ours. His saving grace is freely offered. His pardon is given to all who will receive it.... Not one sinner need be lost. Full and free is the gift of saving grace."[24]

---

[23] E. G. White, *The Messenger,* May 10, 1893, par. 1.

[24] E. G. White, *God's Amazing Grace* (1973), p.179.5.

The Most Precious Message

104

13. *The Third Angel's Message & the Loud Cry*

"The love of a holy God is an amazing principle, which can stir the universe in our behalf during the hours of our probation and trial. But after the season of our probation, if we are found transgressors of God's law, the God of love will be found a minister of vengeance. God makes no compromise with sin. The disobedient will be punished. The wrath of God fell upon His beloved Son as Christ hung upon the cross of Calvary in the transgressor's place. The love of God now reaches out to embrace the lowest, vilest sinner that will come to Christ with contrition. It reaches out to transform the sinner into an obedient, faithful child of God; but not a soul can be saved if he continues in sin."[1]

The book of Revelation outlines four specific messages to be given to the world just before the seven last plagues are poured out. The people of God unite in the power of the final outpouring of the Holy Spirit, called the latter rain, to take these messages to the whole world to warn sinners of the coming judgements of God, that all who would may escape the final punishments to be poured on the wicked. "And the third angel followed them, saying with a loud voice, If any man worship the beast and his image, and receive his mark in his forehead, or in his hand, The same shall drink of the wine of the wrath of God, which is poured out without mixture into the cup of his indignation; and he shall be tormented with fire and brimstone in the presence of the holy angels, and in the presence of the Lamb: And the smoke of their torment ascendeth up for ever and ever: and they have no rest day nor night, who worship the beast and his image, and whosoever receiveth the mark of his name. Here is the patience of the saints: here are they that keep the commandments of God, and the faith of Jesus."[2]

"Here are they that keep the commandments of God:"
1. "Thou shalt have no other gods before me.
2. "Thou shalt not make unto thee any graven image, or any likeness of any thing that is in heaven above, or that is in the earth beneath, or that is in the water under the earth: Thou shalt not

---

[1] E. G. White, *Selected Messages* (1958), Vol. 1 p. 313.1.

[2] Revelation 14:9-12

bow down thyself to them, nor serve them: for I the LORD thy God am a jealous God, visiting the iniquity of the fathers upon the children unto the third and fourth generation of them that hate me; And shewing mercy unto thousands of them that love me, and keep my commandments.

3. "Thou shalt not take the name of the LORD thy God in vain; for the LORD will not hold him guiltless that taketh his name in vain.

4. "Remember the sabbath day, to keep it holy. Six days shalt thou labour, and do all thy work: But the seventh day is the sabbath of the LORD thy God: in it thou shalt not do any work, thou, nor thy son, nor thy daughter, thy manservant, nor thy maidservant, nor thy cattle, nor thy stranger that is within thy gates: For in six days the LORD made heaven and earth, the sea, and all that in them is, and rested the seventh day: wherefore the LORD blessed the sabbath day, and hallowed it.

5. "Honour thy father and thy mother: that thy days may be long upon the land which the LORD thy God giveth thee.

6. "Thou shalt not kill.

7. "Thou shalt not commit adultery.

8. "Thou shalt not steal.

9. "Thou shalt not bear false witness against thy neighbour.

10. "Thou shalt not covet thy neighbour's house, thou shalt not covet thy neighbour's wife, nor his manservant, nor his maidservant, nor his ox, nor his ass, nor any thing that is thy neighbour's."[3]

"The most fearful threatening ever addressed to mortals is contained in the third angel's message. That must be a terrible sin which calls down the wrath of God unmingled with mercy. Men are not to be left in darkness concerning this important matter; the warning against this sin is to be given to the world before the visitation of God's judgments, that all may know why they are to be inflicted, and have opportunity to escape them. Prophecy declares that the first angel would make his announcement to 'every nation, and kindred, and tongue, and people.' The warning of the third angel, which forms a part of the same threefold message, is to be no less widespread. It is represented in the prophecy as being proclaimed with a loud voice, by an angel flying in the midst of heaven; and it will command the attention of the world."[4] "This is the message given by God to be

---

[3] Exodus 20:3-17

[4] E. G. White, *The Great Controversy* (1911), p. 449.2.

sounded forth in the loud cry of the third angel. The sign or seal of God is the observance of the seventh-day Sabbath, and the Lord's memorial of his work of creation. 'The Lord spake unto Moses saying, Speak thou also unto the children of Israel, saying, Verily my Sabbaths ye shall keep: for it is a sign between me and you throughout your generations; that ye may know that I am Lord that doth sanctify you.' Here the Sabbath is clearly defined as a sign between God and his people."[5]

"This thundering message is to be given to an impenitent world, just before Jesus comes. God is not willing that any should perish. This final call is to be made before he pours out his wrath on those that receive the mark of the beast. God warns us in no uncertain terms not to receive the mark of the beast, for if you do you will suffer the wrath of God, which is poured out without mixture—without dilution— or no longer mixed with mercy. Yet God, in his mercy, is revealing here the critical information necessary to identify the mark of the beast and how it may be avoided. If we are to avoid receiving this mark, it is imperative that we know what it is. Revelation 13 provide[s] the framework for the identification of the mark of the beast. 'And he had power to give life unto the image of the beast, that the image of the beast should both speak, and cause that as many as would not worship the image of the beast should be killed.'[6] "Protestant America, represented by the lamb-like beast,[7] will give life unto the image of the beast—the system of false worship legislated by the illegitimate union of church and state. A decree is finally passed that any who will not worship the image of the beast should be killed. Worship is the the central issue in the reception of the mark of the beast. In Revelation 13, the word worship is repeated several times revealing Satan's plan to cause the whole world to worship himself. By worshiping the image of the beast they will worship the beast and by worshiping the beast they worship the devil. In Revelation 14 the issue of worship is repeated again, with the call given to worship God, the Creator of all things, and a warning

---

[5] E. G. White, *Pamphlet 86* (1898), p. 6.1.

[6] Revelation 13:15

[7] See Revelation 13:11-12.

being pronounced against worshiping the beast or anything with which it is connected."[8]

To heed the warning to refuse the mark of the beast, it is necessary to identify the beast. In Revelation 13 "is described another beast, 'like unto a leopard,' to which the dragon gave 'his power, and his seat, and great authority.' This symbol, as most Protestants have believed, represents the papacy, which succeeded to the power and seat and authority once held by the ancient Roman empire. Of the leopardlike beast it is declared: 'There was given unto him a mouth speaking great things and blasphemies.... And he opened his mouth in blasphemy against God, to blaspheme His name, and His tabernacle, and them that dwell in heaven. And it was given unto him to make war with the saints, and to overcome them: and power was given him over all kindreds, and tongues, and nations.' This prophecy, which is nearly identical with the description of the little horn of Daniel 7, unquestionably points to the papacy."[9]

The papacy claims the change of the day of worship from the seventh-day Sabbath to Sunday as the mark of their authority. The following quotes demonstrate this bold claim from Catholic sources: "I have repeatedly offered $1,000 to any one who can prove to me from the Bible alone that I am bound to keep Sunday holy. There is no such law in the Bible. It is a law of the holy Catholic Church alone. The Bible says, 'Remember that thou keep holy the Sabbath day.' The Catholic Church says: 'No! By my divine power I abolish the Sabbath day, and command you to keep holy the first day of the week.' And, lo! the entire civilized world bows down in reverent obedience to the command of the holy Catholic Church. Yours respectfully, T. ENRIGHT, CSS. R."[10] "If protestants would follow the Bible, they should worship God on the Sabbath day. In keeping the Sunday, they are following a law of the Catholic

---

[8] Martin Klein, *Glimpses of the Open Gates of Heaven*, p. 579-580.

[9] E. G. White, *The Great Controversy* (1911), p. 439.1.
For more information on the Biblical identification of the beast as the papal power seated at Rome see Martin Klein, *Glimpses of the Open Gates of Heaven*, A Verse by Verse Study of the Books of Daniel and Revelation.

[10] Fr. Enright, CSS. R. to E.E. Franke, January 11, 1892, in "An Adventist Minister on Sunday Laws," *American Sentinel*, June 1, 1893, p. 173.

Church."[11] "Protestantism, in disregarding the authority of the Roman [Catholic] Church, has no good reason for its Sunday theory and ought logically to keep Saturday as the Sabbath."[12] "Reason and common sense demand the acceptance of one or the other of these alternatives: either Protestantism and the keeping holy of Saturday. Or Catholicity and the keeping holy of Sunday. Compromise is impossible."[13]

"The Sabbath is the sign of God; it is the seal of his law. Isaiah 8:16 It is the token of his authority and power. It is a sign whereby we may know that he is God, and therefore it is appropriately said to be placed in the forehead. The worshipers of the beast (Revelation 13) are said to receive his mark in their foreheads or in their hands. As the forehead represents the intellect, the hand represents power. Psalms 89:48, 'Shall he deliver his soul from the hand of the grave?' Compulsory worship is not acceptable to God; his servants are sealed only in their foreheads. But it is acceptable to wicked powers; it has always been craved by the Romish hierarchy.... The sign or seal of God is his Sabbath, and the seal or mark of the beast is in direct opposition to it; it is a counterfeit Sabbath on the 'day of the sun.' In the message of the third angel (Revelation 14:9-12) they who do not receive the mark of the beast keep the commandments of God, and the Sabbath is in the fourth precept; they keep the Sabbath of the Lord; they have his sign or seal. The importance of this sign is shown in this, that the fourth commandment is the only one in the law which distinguishes the Creator from false gods. Compare Jeremiah 10:10-12; Acts 17:23, 24; Revelation 14:6, 7; etc. And it is that part of his law for keeping which his people will suffer persecution. But when the wrath of God comes upon the persecutors who are found enforcing the sign or mark of the beast, then they will realize the importance of the Sabbath—the seal of the living God. They who turn away from that which the Lord spoke when his voice shook the earth, will confess their fatal error when his voice shall shake the heavens and the earth. Hebrews 12:25, 26: Joel 3:9-16,

---

[11] Albert Smith, Chancellor of Archdiocese of Baltimore, replying for the cardinal in a letter dated February 10, 1920.

[12] John Gilmary Shea, L.L.D., *American Catholic Quarterly Review*, Vol. 8—January, 1883—No. 29 (Philadelphia: Hardy & Mahony, Publishers and Proprietors, 1883), p. 152.

[13] "The Christian Sabbath," *The Catholic Mirror*, December 23, 1893, p. 8-9.

and others."[14] "The Sabbath will be the great test of loyalty, for it is the point of truth especially controverted. When the final test shall be brought to bear upon men, then the line of distinction will be drawn between those who serve God and those who serve Him not. While the observance of the false sabbath in compliance with the law of the state, contrary to the fourth commandment, will be an avowal of allegiance to a power that is in opposition to God, the keeping of the true Sabbath, in obedience to God's law, is an evidence of loyalty to the Creator. While one class, by accepting the sign of submission to earthly powers, receive the mark of the beast, the other, choosing the token of allegiance to divine authority, receive the seal of God."[15]

"The Lord commands.... 'Bind up the testimony, seal the law among My disciples.' Isaiah 8:16. The seal of God's law is found in the fourth commandment. This only, of all the ten, brings to view both the name and the title of the Lawgiver. It declares Him to be the Creator of the heavens and the earth, and thus shows His claim to reverence and worship above all others. Aside from this precept, there is nothing in the Decalogue to show by whose authority the law is given. When the Sabbath was changed by the papal power, the seal was taken from the law. The disciples of Jesus are called upon to restore it by exalting the Sabbath of the fourth commandment to its rightful position as the Creator's memorial and the sign of His authority."[16]

"No one has yet received the mark of the beast. The testing time has not yet come. There are true Christians in every church, not excepting the Roman Catholic communion. None are condemned until they have had the light and have seen the obligation of the fourth commandment. But when the decree shall go forth enforcing the counterfeit sabbath, and the loud cry of the third angel shall warn men against the worship of the beast and his image, the line will be clearly drawn between the false and the true. Then those who still continue in transgression will receive the mark of the beast.

"With rapid steps we are approaching this period. When Protestant churches shall unite with the secular power to sustain a false religion, for opposing which their ancestors endured the fiercest persecution, then will the papal sabbath be enforced by the

---

[14] E. G. White, *The Spirit of Prophecy* (1884), Vol. 4, p. 505.3.

[15] E. G. White, *The Great Controversy* (1911), p. 605.2.

[16] *Ibid.*, p. 452.1.

combined authority of church and state. There will be a national apostasy, which will end only in national ruin."[17]

"If the light of truth has been presented to you, revealing the Sabbath of the fourth commandment, and showing that there is no foundation in the Word of God for Sunday observance, and yet you still cling to the false sabbath, refusing to keep holy the Sabbath which God calls "my holy day," you receive the mark of the beast. When does this take place? When you obey the decree that commands you to cease from labor on Sunday and worship God, while you know that there is not a word in the Bible showing Sunday to be other than a common working day, you consent to receive the mark of the beast, and refuse the seal of God."[18]

"The world is preparing for the closing work of the third angel's message. The truth is now to go forth with a power that it has not known for years. The message of present truth is to be proclaimed everywhere. We must be aroused to give this message with a loud voice, as symbolized in the fourteenth chapter of Revelation. There is danger of our accepting the theory of the truth without accepting the great responsibility which it lays upon every recipient. My brethren, show your faith by your works. The world must be prepared for the loud cry of the third angel's message—a message which God declares shall be cut short in righteousness."[19]

"John was called to behold a people distinct from those who worship the beast or his image by keeping the first day of the week. The observance of this day is the mark of the beast. John declares, 'Here is the patience of the saints: here are they that keep the commandments of God, and the faith of Jesus.'"[20] "As foretold in the eighteenth of Revelation, the third angel's message is to be

[17] E. G. White, *Evangelism* (Washington, D.C.: Review and Herald Publishing Association, 1946), p. 234.2-235.1.

[18] E. G. White, *Maranatha* (Washington, D.C.: Review and Herald Publishing Association, 1976), p. 211.6.

[19] E. G. White, *Manuscript Releases* (1990), Vol. 10, p. 218.3.

[20] E. G. White, *Testimonies to Ministers and Gospel Workers* (1923), p. 133.1.

proclaimed with great power by those who give the final warning against the beast and his image."[21]

"The time of test is just upon us, for the loud cry of the third angel has already begun in the revelation of the righteousness of Christ, the sin-pardoning Redeemer. This is the beginning of the light of the angel whose glory shall fill the whole earth. For it is the work of every one to whom the message of warning has come, to lift up Jesus, to present Him to the world as revealed in types, as shadowed in symbols, as manifested in the revelations of the prophets, as unveiled in the lessons given to His disciples and in the wonderful miracles wrought for the sons of men. Search the Scriptures; for they are they that testify of Him."[22] "If we would have the spirit and power of the third angel's message, we must present the law and the gospel together, for they go hand in hand. As a power from beneath is stirring up the children of disobedience to make void the law of God, and to trample upon the faith of Christ as our righteousness, a power from above is moving upon the hearts of those who are loyal, to exalt the law, and to lift up Jesus as a complete Saviour. Unless divine power is brought into the experience of the people of God, false theories and erroneous ideas will take minds captive, Christ and his righteousness will be dropped out of the experience of many, and their faith will be without power or life. Such will not have a daily, living experience of the love of God in the heart; and if they do not zealously repent, they will be among those who are represented by the Laodiceans, who will be spewed out of the mouth of God."[23]

"When the storm of persecution really breaks upon us, the true sheep will hear the true Shepherd's voice. Self-denying efforts will be put forth to save the lost, and many who have strayed from the fold will come back to follow the great Shepherd.... The love of Christ, the love of our brethren, will testify to the world that we have been with Jesus and learned of Him. Then will the message of the third angel swell to a loud cry, and the whole earth will be lightened with the glory of the Lord."[24]

---

[21] E. G. White, *Last Day Events* (1992), p. 201.6.

[22] E. G. White, *Prophets and Kings* (Mountain View, CA: Pacific Press Publishing Association, 1917), p. 174.3.

[23] E. G. White, *Gospel Workers* (1915), p. 103.3.

[24] E. G. White, *Evangelism* (1946), p. 693.2.

"Some of our brethren have expressed fears that we shall dwell too much upon the subject of justification by faith, but I hope and pray that none will be needlessly alarmed; for there is no danger in presenting this doctrine as it is set forth in the Scriptures. If there had not been a remissness in the past to properly instruct the people of God, there would not now be a necessity of calling a special attention to it.... The exceeding great and precious promises given us in the Holy Scriptures have been lost sight of to a great extent, just as the enemy of all righteousness designed that they should be. He has cast his own dark shadow between us and our God, that we may not see the true character of God. The Lord has proclaimed Himself to be 'merciful and gracious, long-suffering, and abundant in goodness and truth.'

"Several have written to me, inquiring if the message of justification by faith is the third angel's message, and I have answered, 'It is the third angel's message, in verity.'"[25]

How is the third angel's message, which is a warning to refuse the mark of the beast, the message of justification by faith? The command to avoid the mark of the beast is a command not to worship on Sunday, the papal sabbath. Therefore, the command to avoid the mark of the beast is really a call to obey God's commandments by worshipping on his holy day, the seventh-day sabbath. More broadly it is an injunction to keep all of God's commandments: "here are they that keep the commandments of God, and the faith of Jesus."[26] But without the power and righteousness of Christ this is not possible, for "without me ye can do nothing."[27] Even our best efforts to keep God's law are tainted with sin, for "all our righteousnesses are as filthy rags."[28] Although God commands and therefore expects us to keep his law, it is not by the keeping of the law that we are saved, for "by the deeds of the law there shall no flesh be justified in his sight: for by the law is the knowledge of sin."[29] Only by faith in the perfect life of Christ and his infinite sacrifice on the cross can we stand; only by his faith replacing

---

[25] E. G. White, *Selected Messages* (1958), Vol. 1, p. 372.1-2.

[26] Revelation 14:12

[27] John 15:5

[28] Isaiah 64:6

[29] Romans 3:20

our faltering belief may we be justified in his sight, and attain salvation, "for the wages of sin is death; but the gift of God is eternal life through Jesus Christ our Lord."[30] Therefore it is only the power and righteousness of Christ that will enable us to keep God's commandments instead of receiving the mark of the beast. "Now unto him that is able to keep you from falling, and to present you faultless before the presence of his glory with exceeding joy, To the only wise God our Saviour, be glory and majesty, dominion and power, both now and for ever. Amen."[31]

"The Lord desires to see the work of proclaiming the third Angel's message carried forward with increasing efficiency. As He has worked in all ages to give victories to His people, so in this age He longs to carry to a triumphant fulfillment His purposes for His church. He bids His believing saints to advance unitedly, going from strength to greater strength, from faith to increased assurance and confidence in the truth and righteousness of His cause.

"We are to stand firm as a rock to the principles of the word of God, remembering that God is with us to give us strength to meet each new experience. Let us ever maintain in our lives the principles of righteousness, that we may go forward from strength to strength in the name of the Lord. We are to hold as very sacred the faith that has been substantiated by the instruction and approval of the Spirit of God from our earliest experience until the present time. We are to cherish as very precious the work that the Lord has been carrying forward through His commandment-keeping people, and which, through the power of His grace, will grow stronger and more efficient as time advances. The enemy is seeking to becloud the discernment of God's people, and to weaken their efficiency; but if they will labor as the Spirit of God shall direct, He will open doors of opportunity before them for the work of building up the old waste places. Their experience will be one of constant growth, until the Lord shall descend from heaven with power and great glory to set His seal of final triumph upon His faithful ones.

"The work that lies before us is one that will put to the stretch every power of the human being. It will call for the exercise of strong faith and constant vigilance. At times the difficulties that we shall meet will be most disheartening. The very greatness of the task will appall us.

---

[30] Romans 6:23

[31] Jude 1:25

And yet, with God's help, His servants will finally triumph. 'Wherefore,' my brethren, 'I desire that ye faint not' because of the trying experiences that are before you. Jesus will be with you; He will go before you by His Holy Spirit, preparing the way; and He will be your helper in every emergency."[32]

"Now unto Him that is able to do exceeding abundantly above all that we ask or think, according to the power that worketh in us, unto Him be glory in the church by Christ Jesus throughout all ages, world without end. Amen."[33]

---

[32] E. G. White, *Councils for the Church* (Nampa, ID: Pacific Press Publishing Association, 1991), p. 357.1-4.

[33] Ephesians 3:20, 21

14. The Outpouring of the Holy Spirit

Scripture describes God as one God,[1] consisting of three individuals —the Father, the Son, and the Holy Spirit,[2] with all three beings present at each of the most important occasions of the history of our world. This union of three divine persons is referred to in the Bible as the Godhead.[3] "For there are three that bear record in heaven, the Father, the Word, and the Holy Ghost: and these three are one."[4]

At the creation of this planet all three members of the Godhead were present: "And the earth was without form, and void; and darkness was upon the face of the deep. And the Spirit of God moved upon the face of the waters."[5] "And God said, **Let us** make man in our image, after our likeness: and let them have dominion over the fish of the sea, and over the fowl of the air, and over the cattle, and over all the earth, and over every creeping thing that creepeth upon the earth."[6] "In the beginning was the Word, and the Word was with God, and the Word was God. The same was in the beginning with God. All things were made by him; and without him was not any thing made that was made.... And the Word was made flesh, and dwelt among us, (and we beheld his glory, the glory as of the only begotten of the Father,) full of grace and truth."[7]

---

[1] Deuteronomy 6:4 Hear, O Israel: The LORD our God is one LORD.

[2] "We need to realize that the Holy Spirit, who is as much a person as God is a person, is walking through these grounds." E. G. White, *Manuscript 66, 1899.*

"The Holy Spirit is a person, for He beareth witness with our spirits that we are the children of God. When this witness is borne, it carries with it its own evidence. At such times we believe and are sure that we are the children of God....
"The Holy Spirit has a personality, else He could not bear witness to our spirits and with our spirits that we are the children of God. He must also be a divine person, else He could not search out the secrets which lie hidden in the mind of God. 'For what man knoweth the things of a man, save the spirit of man which is in him? even so the things of God knoweth no man, but the Spirit of God.'" E. G. White, *Manuscript 20, 1906.*

[3] Colossians 2:8-9 Beware lest any man spoil you through philosophy and vain deceit, after the tradition of men, after the rudiments of the world, and not after Christ. For in him dwelleth all the fulness of the Godhead bodily.

[4] 1 John 5:7

[5] Genesis 1:2

[6] Genesis 1:26

[7] John 1:1-3; 14

At the baptism of Jesus all three members of the Godhead were present: "And **Jesus**, when he was baptized, went up straightway out of the water: and, lo, the heavens were opened unto him, and he saw **the Spirit** of God descending like a dove, and lighting upon him: And lo **a voice from heaven** [the father], saying, This is my beloved Son, in whom I am well pleased."[8]

The great commission commands that all new believers be baptized in all three names: "Go ye therefore, and teach all nations, baptizing them in the name of the Father, and of the Son, and of the Holy Ghost: Teaching them to observe all things whatsoever I have commanded you: and, lo, I am with you alway, even unto the end of the world. Amen."[9]

Jesus promised that when he left the world the Father would send the Comforter, also referred to as the Holy Spirit or Holy Ghost, to teach us all things: "But the Comforter, which is the Holy Ghost, whom the Father will send in my name, he shall teach you all things, and bring all things to your remembrance, whatsoever I have said unto you."[10] "Nevertheless I tell you the truth; It is expedient for you that I go away: for if I go not away, the Comforter will not come unto you; but if I depart, I will send him unto you."[11] "And it shall come to pass afterward, that I will pour out my spirit upon all flesh; and your sons and your daughters shall prophesy, your old men shall dream dreams, your young men shall see visions: And also upon the servants and upon the handmaids in those days will I pour out my spirit. And I will show wonders in the heavens and in the earth, blood, and fire, and pillars of smoke. The sun shall be turned into darkness, and the moon into blood, before the great and the terrible day of the LORD come."[12]

"Near the close of earth's harvest, a special bestowal of spiritual grace is promised to prepare the church for the coming of the Son of man. This outpouring of the Spirit is likened to the falling of the latter

---

[8] Matthew 3:16-17

[9] Matthew 28:20

[10] John 14:26

[11] John 16:7

[12] Joel 2:28-31

rain; and it is for this added power that Christians are to send their petitions to the Lord of the harvest 'in the time of the latter rain.' In response, 'the Lord shall make bright clouds, and give them showers of rain.' 'He will cause to come down... the rain, the former rain, and the latter rain,' Zechariah 10:1; Joel 2:23.

"But unless the members of God's church today have a living connection with the Source of all spiritual growth, they will not be ready for the time of reaping. Unless they keep their lamps trimmed and burning, they will fail of receiving added grace in times of special need.

"Those only who are constantly receiving fresh supplies of grace, will have power proportionate to their daily need and their ability to use that power. Instead of looking forward to some future time when, through a special endowment of spiritual power, they will receive a miraculous fitting up for soul winning, they are yielding themselves daily to God, that He may make them vessels meet for His use. Daily they are improving the opportunities for service that lie within their reach. Daily they are witnessing for the Master wherever they may be, whether in some humble sphere of labor in the home, or in a public field of usefulness."[13]

"It is true that in the time of the end, when God's work in the earth is closing, the earnest efforts put forth by consecrated believers under the guidance of the Holy Spirit are to be accompanied by special tokens of divine favor. Under the figure of the early and the latter rain, that falls in Eastern lands at seedtime and harvest, the Hebrew prophets foretold the bestowal of spiritual grace in extraordinary measure upon God's church. The outpouring of the Spirit in the days of the apostles was the beginning of the early, or former, rain, and glorious was the result. To the end of time the presence of the Spirit is to abide with the true church.

"'He will cause to come down for you the rain, the former rain, and the latter rain.' In the East the former rain falls at the sowing time. It is necessary in order that the seed may germinate. Under the influence of the fertilizing showers the tender shoot springs up. The latter rain, falling near the close of the season, ripens the grain and prepares it for the sickle. The Lord employs these operations of nature to represent the work of the Holy Spirit. [See Zechariah 10:1; Hosea 6:3; Joel 2:23, 28.]

---

[13] E. G. White, *The Acts of the Apostles* (1911), p. 54.2-55.3.

"As the dew and the rain are given first to cause the seed to germinate, and then to ripen the harvest, so the Holy Spirit is given to carry forward, from one stage to another, the process of spiritual growth. The ripening of the grain represents the completion of the work of God's grace in the soul. By the power of the Holy Spirit the moral image of God is to be perfected in the character. We are to be wholly transformed into the likeness of Christ.

"The latter rain, ripening earth's harvest, represents the spiritual grace that prepares the church for the coming of the Son of man. But unless the former rain has fallen, there will be no life; the green blade will not spring up. Unless the early showers have done their work, the latter rain can bring no seed to perfection."[14]

"The outpouring of the Spirit in the days of the apostles was 'the former rain,' and glorious was the result. But the latter rain will be more abundant."[15]

"At no point in our experience can we dispense with the assistance of that which enables us to make the first start. The blessings received under the former rain are needful to us to the end. . . . As we seek God for the Holy Spirit, it will work in us meekness, humbleness of mind, a conscious dependence upon God for the perfecting latter rain.

"The Holy Spirit seeks to abide in each soul. If it is welcomed as an honored guest, those who receive it will be made complete in Christ. The good work begun will be finished; the holy thoughts, heavenly affections, and Christlike actions will take the place of impure thoughts, perverse sentiments, and rebellious acts.

"We may have had a measure of the Spirit of God, but by prayer and faith we are continually to seek more of the Spirit. It will never do to cease our efforts. If we do not progress, if we do not place ourselves in an attitude to receive both the former and the latter rain, we shall lose our souls, and the responsibility will lie at our own door....

"The convocations of the church, as in camp meetings, the assemblies of the home church, and all occasions where there is personal labor for souls, are God's appointed opportunities for giving the early and the latter rain.

---

[14] E. G. White, *Last Day Events* (1992), p. 183.1-3.

[15] *Ibid.*, p. 185.5.

"When the way is prepared for the Spirit of God, the blessing will come. Satan can no more hinder a shower of blessing from descending upon God's people than he can close the windows of heaven that rain cannot come upon the earth."[16]

"Are we hoping to see the whole church revived? That time will never come. There are persons in the church who are not converted, and who will not unite in earnest, prevailing prayer. We must enter upon the work individually. We must pray more, and talk less.
"We may be sure that when the Holy Spirit is poured out, those who did not receive and appreciate the early rain will not see or understand the value of the latter rain.
"Only those who are living up to the light they have will receive greater light. Unless we are daily advancing in the exemplification of the active Christian virtues, we shall not recognize the manifestations of the Holy Spirit in the latter rain. It may be falling on hearts all around us, but we shall not discern or receive it.
"Those who make no decided effort, but simply wait for the Holy Spirit to compel them to action, will perish in darkness. You are not to sit still and do nothing in the work of God."[17]

"A revival of true godliness among us is the greatest and most urgent of all our needs. To seek this should be our first work. There must be earnest effort to obtain the blessing of the Lord, not because God is not willing to bestow His blessing upon us, but because we are unprepared to receive it. Our heavenly Father is more willing to give His Holy Spirit to them that ask Him, than are earthly parents to give good gifts to their children. But it is our work, by confession, humiliation, repentance, and earnest prayer, to fulfill the conditions upon which God has promised to grant us His blessing. A revival need be expected only in answer to prayer."[18]

"The Holy Spirit is Christ's representative, but divested of the personality of humanity, and independent thereof. Cumbered with humanity, Christ could not be in every place personally. Therefore it was for their interest that He should go to the Father, and send the

---

[16] E. G. White, *Last Day Events* (1992), p. 187.1-188.2.

[17] *Ibid.*, p. 195.1-196.1.

[18] *Ibid.*, p. 189.1

Spirit to be His successor on earth. No one could then have any advantage because of his location or his personal contact with Christ. By the Spirit the Saviour would be accessible to all. In this sense He would be nearer to them than if He had not ascended on high."[19]

"Let every one who claims to believe that the Lord is soon coming, search the Scriptures as never before; for Satan is determined to try every device possible to keep souls in darkness, and blind the mind to the perils of the times in which we are living. Let every believer take up his Bible with earnest prayer, that he may be enlightened by the Holy Spirit as to what is truth, that he may know more of God and of Jesus Christ whom He has sent. Search for the truth as for hidden treasures, and disappoint the enemy."[20]

"The glad tidings of a risen Saviour were carried [by the disciples] to the uttermost bounds of the inhabited world. The church beheld converts flocking to her from all directions. Believers were reconverted. Sinners united with Christians in seeking the pearl of great price. The prophecy was fulfilled, The weak shall be 'as David,' and the house of David 'as the angel of the Lord.' Zechariah 12:8. Every Christian saw in his brother the divine similitude of benevolence and love. One interest prevailed. One object swallowed up all others. All hearts beat in harmony. The only ambition of the believers was to reveal the likeness of Christ's character, and to labor for the enlargement of His kingdom. 'The multitude of them that believed were of one heart and of one soul.... With great power gave the apostles witness of the resurrection of the Lord Jesus; and great grace was upon them all.' Acts 4:32, 33. 'And the Lord added to the church daily such as should be saved.' Acts 2:47. The Spirit of Christ animated the whole congregation; for they had found the pearl of great price.
"These scenes are to be repeated, and with greater power. The outpouring of the Holy Spirit on the day of Pentecost was the former rain, but the latter rain will be more abundant. The Spirit awaits our demand and reception. Christ is again to be revealed in His fullness by the Holy Spirit's power. Men will discern the value of the precious pearl, and with the apostle Paul they will say, 'What things were gain

---

[19] E. G. White, *The Desire of Ages* (1898), p. 669.

[20] E. G. White, *Selected Messages* (1958), Vol. 1, p. 362.4.

to me, those I counted loss for Christ. Yea doubtless, and I count all things but loss for the excellency of the knowledge of Christ Jesus my Lord.'"[21]

"Revelation 18 points to the time when, as the result of rejecting the threefold warning of Revelation 14:6-12, the church will have fully reached the condition foretold by the second angel, and the people of God still in Babylon will be called upon to separate from her communion. This message is the last that will ever be given to the world."[22]

"I saw another angel come down from heaven, having great power; and the earth was lightened with his glory. And he cried mightily with a strong voice, saying, Babylon the great is fallen, is fallen, and is become the habitation of devils, and the hold of every foul spirit, and a cage of every unclean and hateful bird.... And I heard another voice from heaven, saying, Come out of her, my people, that ye be not partakers of her sins, and that ye receive not of her plagues."[23]

"This scripture points forward to a time when the announcement of the fall of Babylon, as made by the second angel of Revelation 14:8, is to be repeated, with the additional mention of the corruptions which have been entering the various organizations that constitute Babylon, since that message was first given, in the summer of 1844... These announcements, uniting with the third angel's message, constitute the final warning to be given to the inhabitants of the earth."[24]

"Thus the message of the third angel will be proclaimed. As the time comes for it to be given with greatest power, the Lord will work through humble instruments, leading the minds of those who consecrate themselves to His service. The laborers will be qualified rather by the unction of His Spirit than by the training of literary institutions. Men of faith and prayer will be constrained to go forth with holy zeal, declaring the words which God gives them. The sins

---

[21] E. G. White, *Christ's Object Lessons* (1900), p. 120.1-121.1.

[22] E. G. White, *The Great Controversy* (1911), p. 390.2

[23] Revelation 18:1, 2, 4

[24] E. G. White, *Last Day Events* (1992), p. 199.1-3.

of Babylon will be laid open. The fearful results of enforcing the observances of the church by civil authority, the inroads of spiritualism, the stealthy but rapid progress of the papal power—all will be unmasked. By these solemn warnings the people will be stirred. Thousands upon thousands will listen who have never heard words like these. In amazement they hear the testimony that Babylon is the church, fallen because of her errors and sins, because of her rejection of the truth sent to her from heaven. As the people go to their former teachers with the eager inquiry, Are these things so? the ministers present fables, prophesy smooth things, to soothe their fears and quiet the awakened conscience. But since many refuse to be satisfied with the mere authority of men and demand a plain 'Thus saith the Lord,' the popular ministry, like the Pharisees of old, filled with anger as their authority is questioned, will denounce the message as of Satan and stir up the sin-loving multitudes to revile and persecute those who proclaim it."[25]

"As the third message swells to a loud cry and as great power and glory attend the closing work, the faithful people of God will partake of that glory. It is the latter rain which revives and strengthens them to pass through the time of trouble.
"As the end approaches, the testimonies of God's servants will become more decided and more powerful.
"This message [Revelation 14:9-12] embraces the two preceding messages. It is represented as being given with a loud voice; that is, with the power of the Holy Spirit."[26]

"At that time the 'latter rain,' or refreshing from the presence of the Lord, will come, to give power to the loud voice of the third angel, and prepare the saints to stand in the period when the seven last plagues shall be poured out."[27] "Before the final visitation of God's judgments upon the earth there will be among the people of the Lord such a revival of primitive godliness as has not been witnessed since apostolic times. The Spirit and power of God will be poured out upon His children.
"The work will be similar to that of the Day of Pentecost. As the 'former rain' was given, in the outpouring of the Holy Spirit at the

[25] E. G. White, *The Great Controversy* (1911), p. 606.2.

[26] E. G. White, *Last Day Events* (1992), p. 201.1-3.

[27] *Ibid.*, p. 186.4-5.

opening of the gospel, to cause the upspringing of the precious seed, so the 'latter rain' will be given at its close for the ripening of the harvest."[28]

We have the privilege to request the gift of the Holy Spirit, which God is longing to give. "And I say unto you, Ask, and it shall be given you; seek, and ye shall find; knock, and it shall be opened unto you. For every one that asketh receiveth; and he that seeketh findeth; and to him that knocketh it shall be opened. If a son shall ask bread of any of you that is a father, will he give him a stone? or if he ask a fish, will he for a fish give him a serpent? Or if he shall ask an egg, will he offer him a scorpion? If ye then, being evil, know how to give good gifts unto your children: how much more shall your heavenly Father give the Holy Spirit to them that ask him?"[29]

The End

---

[28] E. G. White, *Last Day Events* (1992), p. 185.5-186.3.

[29] Luke 11:9-13

The Most Precious Message

126

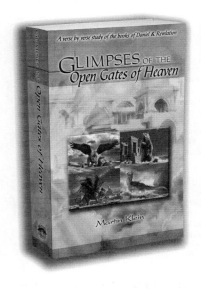

Glimpses of the Open Gates of Heaven: *A verse by verse study of the books of Daniel & Revelation*

The books of Daniel and Revelation have fascinated theologians, archeologists, scientists, historians, monarchs, peasants, and children for millennia. Filled with fascinating symbolic imagery of beasts rising from seething waves; a bloodthirsty dragon chasing a fair maiden; apocalyptic plagues pouring over the planet; cryptic numbers and mysterious predictions; all calling for the curious and the concerned alike to heed the warnings they contain.

"The present is a time of overwhelming interest to all living. Rulers and statesmen, men who occupy positions of trust and authority, thinking men and women of all classes, have their attention fixed upon the events taking place about us. They are watching the relations that exist among the nations. They observe the intensity that is taking possession of every earthly element and they recognize that something great and decisive is about to take place—that the world is on the verge of a stupendous crisis.

"The calamities by land and sea, the unsettled state of society, the alarms of war, are portentous. They forecast approaching events of the greatest magnitude.... Great changes are soon to take place in our world, and the final movements will be rapid ones." In a most dramatic way, the future is laid open in these prophetic pages. These messages will prepare a people to stand in the great day of God.

Paperback: 777 pages
Publisher: Savannah Pictures
ISBN-13: 978-0997589733
ISBN-10: 0997589736
BISAC: Religion / Christian Theology / Eschatology

Download free pdf sample of this book: https://savannahpictures.wistia.com/projects/i25r2uifkm

Thou Hast Magnified Thy Word
Above All Thy Name

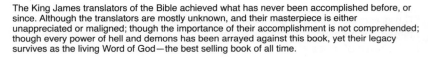

The Bible makes the claim to absolute truthfulness and infallibility.[1] It then provides the internal evidence to verify this claim. Complete harmony through sixty-six books by about forty different writers, spanning one and a half millennia, would be impossible if the author were not the Holy Spirit. In order for Scripture to make the claim of truthfulness, it must also contain the promise of preservation. God's promise to preserve his pure Word is dramatically fulfilled in the 1611 publication of the Authorized Version of the Bible, more commonly known today as the King James Version.

The Bible's power, feared by its enemies, is the power to transform those who submit to its claims, and love its precepts. The written words of the King James translators have had a greater influence on this world than any other literary work the planet has ever seen. It has changed the course of nations, and altered history in a way the translators could not have fathomed. It has transmitted the precious gospel message to more souls than all other agencies combined. Only in eternity will its power be comprehended.

The King James translators of the Bible achieved what has never been accomplished before, or since. Although the translators are mostly unknown, and their masterpiece is either unappreciated or maligned; though the importance of their accomplishment is not comprehended; though every power of hell and demons has been arrayed against this book, yet their legacy survives as the living Word of God—the best selling book of all time.

Though God promised to preserve his word, the stern facts of history and the unyielding testimony of Scripture prove that attempts have been made to pervert God's Word: "ye have perverted the words of the living God," Jeremiah 23:36.

Compare: KJV Job 19:26 "yet in my flesh shall I see God:"
          ASV Job 19:26 "then without my flesh shall I see God;"
Simple logic demands that two opposite statements cannot both be true. Therefore one must be false. The one that is false cannot be God's pure, true, unperverted Word.

Thus, to fulfill the promise of preservation, the Scripture must contain a way to distinguish between the genuine and the counterfeit. With demonstrable and rather serious differences in so many current versions of the Bible, how can we be certain what is God's true and preserved Word? This book answers this question.

Paperback: 254 pages
Publisher: Savannah Pictures
ISBN: 978-0-9975897-0-2 (paperback)
       978-0-9975897-1-9 (e-book)
       978-0-9975897-2-6 (abridged edition)
       978-0-9975897-5-7 (paperback—2nd Edition)
Religion: Christian Theology: Apologetics

Download free pdf sample of this book https://savannahpictures.wistia.com/projects/kkmci6ospk

---

[1] 1 Kings 8:56